500 RECIPES
FOR FAMILIES

---

by Marguerite Patten

HAMLYN

LONDON · NEW YORK · SYDNEY · TORONTO

Contents

Cover photograph by Paul Williams

Published by The Hamlyn Publishing Group Limited
London · New York · Sydney · Toronto
Astronaut House, Feltham, Middlesex, England

© Copyright The Hamlyn Publishing Group Limited 1962

First published 1962
Twentieth impression 1983

ISBN 0 600 03400 3

Printed and bound in Great Britain by R. J. Acford

Introduction

This book has been especially compiled for those of you who run a home and cater for a family. It is first and foremost a *practical* book, but at the same time I have tried to provide as many new, helpful and exciting ideas as possible. But let me tell you something about the book and you will see what I mean. In Chapter 1 you will find hints on helping you run your kitchen economically and well. I have also dealt with such practical problems as how to save money on food and the best ways of keeping it fresh. You will also find ideas for using the left-overs one occasionally finds in every home.

Chapter 2 is devoted to the all-important topic of breakfast, and includes a number of quick, easy and delicious breakfast recipes. Some people rather cheerfully say they never eat breakfast, and it is too often a hurried and unattractive meal. But some kind of breakfast is really rather important, particularly in cold weather and particularly for those members of the family who are going off to school and work.

Families vary. Some people like their main meal in the middle of the day, others in the evening. Whatever your preference, you will find a wide range of interesting recipes in Chapters 3 to 9 which cover the main meal from soup to dessert.

Chapters 10, 11 and 12 are centred around what is perhaps the cosiest and friendliest meal of the day—family tea time. The art of home baking is still very much alive, for I know when giving a demonstration the interest and enthusiasm displayed by housewives when they see a home-made cake come out of the oven! I have therefore tried to make the tea time recipes as varied and interesting as possible. In Chapter 13 you will find snacks, savouries and salads, the kind of light, tasty dish which can be served either for lunch or supper, or as a late evening snack when friends drop in unexpectedly. Chapter 14 includes recipes for sauces and stuffings.

Altogether the book contains hundreds of ideas and recipes (all recipes will serve four people unless otherwise stated). I very much hope they will provide you with friendly help and stimulating ideas throughout the year.

Some Useful Facts and Figures

Notes on metrication

In case you wish to convert quantities into metric measures, the following tables give a comparison.

Solid measures

Ounces	Approx. grams to nearest whole figure	Recommended conversion to nearest unit of 25
1	28	25
2	57	50
3	85	75
4	113	100
5	142	150
6	170	175
7	198	200
8	227	225
9	255	250
10	283	275
11	312	300
12	340	350
13	368	375
14	396	400
15	425	425
16 (1 lb)	454	450
17	482	475
18	510	500
19	539	550
20 (1¼ lb)	567	575

Note: When converting quantities over 20 oz first add the appropriate figures in the centre column, then adjust to the nearest unit of 25. As a general guide, 1 kg (1000 g) equals 2·2 lb or about 2 lb 3 oz. This method of conversion gives good results in nearly all cases, although in certain pastry and cake recipes a more accurate conversion is necessary to produce a balanced recipe.

Liquid measures

Imperial	Approx. millilitres to nearest whole figure	Recommended millilitres
¼ pint	142	150
½ pint	283	300
¾ pint	425	450
1 pint	567	600
1½ pints	851	900
1¾ pints	992	1000 (1 litre)

Oven temperatures

The table below gives recommended equivalents.

	°C	°F	Gas Mark
Very cool	110	225	$\frac{1}{4}$
	120	250	$\frac{1}{2}$
Cool	140	275	1
	150	300	2
Moderate	160	325	3
	180	350	4
Moderately hot	190	375	5
	200	400	6
Hot	220	425	7
	230	450	8
Very hot	240	475	9

Notes for American and Australian users

In America the 8-oz measuring cup is used. In Australia metric measures are now used in conjunction with the standard 250-ml measuring cup. The Imperial pint, used in Britain and Australia, is 20 fl oz, while the American pint is 16 fl oz. It is important to remember that the Australian tablespoon differs from both the British and American tablespoons; the table below gives a comparison. The British standard tablespoon, which has been used throughout this book, holds 17·7 ml, the American 14·2 ml, and the Australian 20 ml. A teaspoon holds approximately 5 ml in all three countries.

Basic Methods of Cooking

Baking—Cooking in dry heat in the oven.

Boiling—Cooking by immersing the food in a pan of liquid, which must be kept boiling gently the whole time.

Braising—Almost a combination of stewing and roasting. Meat is placed on a bed of vegetables with a little liquid surrounding, in a covered vessel, and cooked slowly in the oven.

Casserole—Cooking slowly in the oven in a covered casserole dish—usually meat, rabbit, etc.

Frying—Cooking in a little hot fat in an open pan. Deep frying is cooking by immersion in a deep pan of smoking hot fat.

Grilling—Cooking quickly under a red-hot grill; used for small tender pieces of meat, fish, etc.

Poaching—Cooking gently in water which is just below boiling point; usually eggs or fish.

Pressure Cooking—Cooking at higher temperatures than usual, so that food is cooked much more quickly.

Roasting—Cooking with a little fat in a hot oven. Fat is poured from the baking tin over the meat or poultry from time to time, using a long-handled spoon; this is known as basting.

Simmering—The rate of cooking used for stews—just below boiling point, so that the liquid bubbles gently at the side of the pan.

Steaming—Cooking either in a steamer over a pan of boiling water, or in a basin standing in (but not covered by) boiling water.

Stewing—Cooking slowly until the food is tender. It is done in just enough liquid to cover the food, as the liquid is served with it and should be rich. Stews may be cooked in covered saucepans or casseroles on a hot plate or in the oven—but always at a low temperature.

Chapter 1

Economical Family Cooking

Foods the family need

A well balanced diet is a very important factor in keeping the family fit. Make sure, therefore, you provide them with:

1 Plenty of protein foods—meat, fish, cheese, eggs are first class proteins. Peas, beans, lentils (the pulses) are second class proteins, and it is wise to serve them at the same meal if you haven't a lot of fish or meat available.

2 A reasonable amount of fat (to help them to keep warm in cold weather)—butter, margarine, cooking fats, suet.
Today doctors are inclined to stress the fact that TOO MUCH fat is unwise in our diet, particularly when approaching middle age. Teenagers and schoolchildren often prefer fried foods to any other, but it is wise catering to try other methods of cooking, as too much fried food can cause over-weight and a poor complexion.

3 Milk. An essential food for children and excellent for adults. If not liked as a drink use it in cooking as much as possible.

4 Sugar (sweets, jams, etc.) is a source of energy, and as such must not be omitted from the diet, except when trying to lose weight. Children should be encouraged to clean their teeth after eating sweets and other sugary foods.

5 Bread, cakes and other starchy foods. While it is unwise to 'fill-up' on bread, etc., so that you do not want to eat other foods, a certain amount is important, since it creates a feeling of well-being. Bread and flour also contain the wheat germ which is an important ingredient to eat.

6 Fruit, vegetables, salads. Many of these provide the vitamin that helps to build up resistance to colds, etc. It is easily destroyed by cooking, so remember *not* to overcook vegetables, and to serve raw fruit, salads, etc., as often as possible.

30 ways to use left-overs

Bread

To freshen stale bread:
Quickly dip the loaf in milk or milk and water. Bake in a moderate oven for 5–10 minutes.

To use stale bread:
1 CRUMBS: Make your own crumbs for coating fish etc. Cut the bread into cubes, put on a baking tray and leave in a hot oven until golden brown.
When quite crisp, roll between sheets of greaseproof paper. Or if preferred, you can make the crumbs first, crisp them, and then roll them to make them very fine.
2 CROUTONS: Cut the stale bread into tiny cubes and fry to serve with soup etc.
3 PUDDINGS: See caramel pudding, Danish apple pudding, butterscotch fingers, bread and butter pudding etc. (pages 56, 57, 69, 59).
4 TARTLET CASES: Cut the stale bread into very thin slices. Press into greased patty tins. Bake until crisp.
Use instead of pastry.

Egg yolks

To preserve egg yolks:
They will keep very much better if covered with a little water (cold) to prevent a skin from forming.
5 Add to pancake batters, creamed vegetables.
6 Use the yolks only in egg custards. They are much richer and give a better result.
7 Use diluted with milk or water for coating fish.

Egg whites

To preserve egg whites:
Keep them covered so they do not evaporate.
8 Use in meringues.
9 FRUIT SNOW: Add an egg white to a gill of thick fruit purée. Egg white must be very stiffly beaten.
10 QUICK MOUSSE: Make a blancmange in the usual way, but with only $\frac{3}{4}$ pint of milk. Allow to cool slightly. Add a little extra sugar and 2 stiffly beaten whites.

Cakes

To preserve cakes:
Keep cake in a separate tin from pastry, biscuits or bread.

11 Use plain cakes in trifles.
12 Use plain or fruit cakes as fritters.
Cut into slices.
Dip in a little milk, or egg and milk, and fry. Sprinkle with sugar.
13 Add fine cake crumbs to custard to make a padded pudding. Top with fruit or grated chocolate.

Fish

Be very careful about using left-over fish as it easily goes bad.
14 Add to mashed potato to form fish cakes, kedgeree (see pages 11, 20).
15 Add to diced vegetables, mayonnaise, rice, for salads.

Jelly

16 Whisk lightly, add a little thick cream and use as a decoration for trifles, instead of icing on cakes or with chopped fruit to fill tartlet cases.

Meat

To preserve:
Meat should always be kept well covered when cooked to prevent drying.
17 There are many recipes in this book for using left-over meat (see Hamburgers, Beef Darioles pages 32, 30). Or mince left-over meat until very fine, mix with a little melted butter and seasoning and use as potted meat.

Milk

18 Milk that has become sour can be used for home-made cheese. Strain it through butter muslin then add seasoning and a little butter to the cheese. Or use the sour milk for mixing scones.

Potatoes

19 **Potatoes gratinée**

you will need:

approximately 1–1¼ lb. cooked potatoes	little milk margarine seasoning
2–3 oz. grated cheese	

Cut potatoes in thick slices.
Arrange in a greased pie dish.
Season well and add small amount of margarine to each layer.

Pour over milk, cover top with cheese.
Cook for about 1 hour in a very moderate oven until milk is absorbed and the cheese forms a really thick crust on top.

0 **Potato croquettes:**
Mash left-over potatoes until very smooth.
Mix with yolk of egg and form into finger shapes.
Roll in egg white and crumbs.
Fry until crisp and brown.

1 **Potato cakes:**
Add grated onion or grated cheese or chopped parsley to mashed potatoes.
Form into flat cakes.
Flour lightly and fry until brown.

2 **Duchesse potatoes:**
Add plenty of margarine and egg yolk to mashed potatoes.
Season well.
Pipe into pretty shapes or form into pyramid shapes.
Bake until crisp and brown.

3 **Potatoes Lyonnaise:**
Fry equal quantities of raw, thinly sliced onion and thickly sliced, left-over cooked potatoes until onions are soft and tender.
Tip on to hot dish, garnish with chopped parsley.

Rice

24 Can be used either as a savoury dish, mixing with fried onions, tomatoes etc. as a quick risotto or as a sweet dish.
Blend it with a little thick cream, serve with fruit.
See also recipe for rice meringue (see page 60).

Steamed puddings

25 Can be re-steamed, or cut into slices and fried. Christmas and rich fruit puddings are particularly good like this.

Sandwiches

26 Dip in beaten egg and milk, fry and serve at once.

Vegetables

27 Mixed with mayonnaise or French dressing, they can be used in salads.
28 Or mix with cheese or tomato sauce, cover with mashed potato and serve as a vegetarian Shepherd's pie.
29 Add to curry sauce and heat gently.
30 Blend with either a very thick white sauce or chopped hard-boiled eggs and the thick sauce.
Form into cutlet shapes.
Coat with egg and breadcrumbs and fry.

Give an added flavour

1 Chopped or dried mint is excellent with pea soup, potato soup or spring soup.
2 Grated cheese is perfect with onion or leek soup, mixed vegetable soup, or tomato soup.
3 Chopped chives not only flavour but garnish most vegetable soups and are excellent for potato soup and cauliflower soup.
4 Sage (either chopped fresh sage or home-dried sage) is a lovely garnish with hare or rabbit soup.
5 A beaten egg stirred into a potato or cauliflower soup gives flavour and food value.
6 Try flavouring tomato soups with a good pinch of brown sugar.
7 Chopped fennel should be added to fish soups and a little could be put with lettuce soup.

10 ways to save money on food

1 Use bones to make a first-class stock, which is the basis for many really delicious soups and stews.
2 Buy dried peas, beans or lentils and use them in savoury dishes. They are cheap to buy and an excellent protein food.
3 Make your own jams, and bottle fruit when it is cheap, then during the winter you will have a wonderful selection in your store cupboard.
4 Buy cheap eggs for cooking, and preserve eggs for the winter when they are a reasonable price.
5 Use shredded cabbage, sprouts, grated carrot, swede in salads when lettuce, cucumber and tomatoes are dear.
6 Yeast cookery for home-made bread and buns will save you money (see pages 65 to 67).
7 Plan your menu, whenever possible, so that you can cook a complete meal on the grill, in the oven, or in a steamer or pressure cooker, to save cooking costs.

8 Learn about the cheaper cuts of bacon, such as collar or streaky, so as to use these instead of gammon or back.
9 Grate orange or lemon rind, cover with sugar. Use these to flavour puddings or cakes instead of buying crystallized peel.
10 Grow a selection of herbs in your garden or window-box. They add a delicious flavour to dishes while fresh, and can be dried for winter use.

10 rules for good cooking

1 Always see your hands, tools and utensils are kept scrupulously clean.
2 Assemble all ingredients for a dish before you begin.
3 Clear up as you work.
4 Weigh or measure accurately.
5 Read the recipe very carefully. When it says 'fold' in flour it means a gentle flick of the wrist, not a heavy stirring.
6 Look after your tools when you have finished, dry off metal tins in the oven before putting them away, put your rolling-pin and wooden spoons in a warm place to dry.
7 Buy a few good kitchen tools rather than lots of inferior ones.
8 Learn to use herbs and spices in cooking.
9 Be adventurous—often you save time and money by trying out new foods and new recipes.
10 The first time you try a new recipe, follow directions exactly. Afterwards you can decide on any alterations to suit your family.

To store foods

BISCUITS. In a tin that is absolutely airtight.
BREAD. Either wrapped in a cloth in a ventilated cupboard or drawer or special bread bin.
BUTTER, COOKING FATS ETC. Put in earthenware dishes and stand these in another dish of cold water. Cover with muslin and allow the ends to stand in the cold water. A good tablespoon of salt added to the water helps to keep temperature low. If you have a refrigerator make sure that these are covered for they readily absorb smells from the other foods in the cabinet. Many cabinets have a special place for storing butter etc., so it does not become too hard.
CAKES. Wrapped in foil or in an airtight tin.
CHEESE. There is a great deal of discussion as to whether this becomes too hard in a refrigerator. If you have a special container it can be kept there otherwise in a cheese dish or an airy cupboard. Many of the continental cheeses need slow ripening to be perfect, so do not put these in the refrigerator.
FISH. Never attempt to store fish for any length of time. Even in a refrigerator it should be kept for the minimum period.
MEAT. This should be put into the refrigerator and uncooked meat is better left uncovered. Cooked meat on the other hand should be well wrapped to prevent drying. If you have no refrigerator then cover the meat in muslin, which has been wrung out in a little vinegar and water. If you keep the meat like this it allows the air to circulate.
MILK. If your storage cupboards are warm then undoubtedly you will be well advised to put the milk into saucepans, bringing it *almost* to boiling point. Don't allow the milk to boil for any length of time. You can let the milk cool, then store in wide-topped jugs, covered with damp muslin. If the weather is only moderately hot you can just stand the milk bottles etc., in cold water, or if you have vacuum flasks at home pour the milk into these the moment it arrives.
The refrigerator is the ideal place for storing milk. Again jugs should be covered in hot weather.
VEGETABLES. Either in the correct container of the refrigerator or spread out on a rather cold surface. If you have to store green vegetables overnight sprinkle them very lightly with cold water. Lettuce etc. keeps best in a covered saucepan or biscuit tin.

Chapter 2
Breakfast Dishes

Many people say they cannot eat breakfast but it is very unwise to go out of the house without eating something first thing in the morning, particularly for young people, and where one has to perhaps make a long journey.

The ready prepared cereals provide a light, very good meal with either hot or cold milk.

Some kind of fruit or fruit juice is an excellent start to the day.

Where people do not like a cooked breakfast it may sound a little unusual to suggest cheese but this is both easy to serve and extremely nutritous.

Grapefruit

1 Allow ½ grapefruit for each person.
2 Cut away the pith and skin, loosen each section with a sharp fruit knife so it is easy to eat.
3 Dust lightly with sugar and decorate with Maraschino cherries or sprigs of mint.
4 Grapefruit has a better flavour if served very cold, so if you have a refrigerator chill before serving.
5 If using canned instead of fresh grapefruit serve in glasses topped with cherries.

Porridge
(with quick cooking oats)

cooking time depending on type of oats used

you will need:

2 cups quick cooking rolled oats	5 cups milk or water salt to taste

1 Add rolled oats (and salt to taste) to boiling milk or water.
2 Boil for 50–60 seconds, stirring continuously if using milk.
3 When water is used stir occasionally.
4 Turn off heat, cover and allow to stand for 5 minutes.
5 Stir and serve.
6 For thicker porridge use more oats.
7 For thinner porridge use less oats.
8 For creamier, smoother porridge, boil for 2 or more minutes, stirring as necessary.

Porridge (with oatmeal)

you will need:

2 tablespoons medium or coarse oatmeal good pinch salt	1 gill cold water 1 pint boiling water

1 Blend the oatmeal with the cold water in the saucepan, stirring well.
2 Gradually add the boiling water and the salt.
3 Put over a fairly high heat and stir until the mixture comes to the boil..

4 Continue stirring for about 5 minutes until the porridge has thickened well.
5 Put a lid on the saucepan, lower the heat and cook gently for 30 minutes.
6 Obviously if you prefer this type of porridge you must get it cooking before attending to anything else for breakfast, or partly cook it the night before, then just warm it through gently the next day.
DOUBLE SAUCEPAN FOR PORRIDGE. To save stirring the porridge you may like to make it in a double saucepan. Mix the porridge in the upper container, fill the bottom pan with boiling water, or allow water to come to the boil. Allow about twice the usual cooking time.

Cooking bacon
Fried bacon

1 Back, streaky, collar or gammon rashers are all recommended for frying. If you want thin rashers ask for a No. 3 cut; gammon rashers, however, are usually cut a little thicker.
2 Cut off the rind with kitchen scissors; this is often useful for your stockpot when making soup. When using streaky bacon be sure to cut off the bone on the other side of the rasher also. If the bacon is very fat, snip the fat through at intervals so that it lies flat when cooking.
3 Put the bacon into a COLD frying pan. Arrange the rashers of bacon so that the lean overlaps the fat. This means that the lean is kept moist and well 'basted' by the fat.
4 There is no need to add fat to the pan as the bacon will make its own, unless it is very lean.

Grilled bacon

1 If you prefer to grill bacon choose just the same cuts as for frying.

2 Cook under a fairly hot grill.
3 Use the grid of the grill pan, and mushrooms, tomatoes etc. can be cooked in the pan below.
4 It may be necessary to start cooking the mushrooms and tomatoes ahead of time, with a knob of butter or margarine, and when half cooked to put under the grill with the bacon on top. In most cookers they should then be ready to serve together.

Bacon and mushrooms

cooking time   10–15 minutes

Fry bacon. Add a little extra fat if necessary before cooking mushrooms or grill them in a pan while bacon is on the grid.

Bacon and sausages

Cook sausages first, either grilling or frying these before cooking bacon.

Bacon and tomatoes

Cook tomatoes after bacon and eggs, since they tend to make the pan sticky. When grilling, the tomatoes can be put in pan under the bacon. Canned peeled tomatoes are excellent with bacon.

Boiled eggs

Most people like their eggs just set, in which case whey will take $3\frac{1}{2}$ minutes. Allow 4 minutes if you know the eggs are very fresh. An egg required to be rather under-set and liquid should have about 3 minutes. A very firm egg, i.e. hard-boiled, needs about 7–10 minutes.
1 Put enough water into a small saucepan to cover the eggs.
2 Bring this to the boil then lower the eggs into the boiling water.
3 If you find one of the egg shells cracking, immediately put about 1 tablespoon vinegar into the water; this prevents the egg coming out of the shell and spoiling.
4 Time carefully and serve at once. Adjust the cooking time according to personal taste.
5 When hard-boiled eggs are cooked, crack shells, lower immediately into cold water. This prevents a dark ring round the yolk.

Fried eggs

1 First cook bacon so that you have bacon fat. Or if not cooking bacon first heat a good knob of fat in the pan.
2 Break the eggs, one by one, into saucers, tilt the pan slightly, put in the egg and cook steadily until set.
3 Repeat this with each egg making sure the

first one is lightly set before the second one goes in.

Economical egg fingers

1 Beat eggs well. Allow 1 for 2 people.
2 Season.
3 Dip fingers of bread into beaten egg, making sure it is thoroughly absorbed.
4 Fry in hot fat.

Poached eggs

Like all egg dishes poached eggs must be served the moment they are cooked, so it is advisable to toast the bread while they cook. Crack the shells and pour the eggs into a cup or saucer.

Method 1. If you have a proper egg-poacher put a piece of margarine or butter, about the size of a hazel nut, into each cup, wait until this is melted, then carefully slide the egg into the cup, adding a pinch of salt if wished. Put on the lid and allow the water in the pan underneath to boil steadily for about $3\frac{1}{2}$–4 minutes. Slide the egg on to the buttered toast.

Method 2. Put a small piece of margarine or butter into an old cup and stand it in a pan of boiling water to melt. Pour in egg, put a lid on saucepan and cook as before.

Method 3. (Preferred by many people since it gives a lighter result.) Bring a good $\frac{1}{2}$ pint of water to the boil in either a saucepan or frying pan.

Add 1 dessertspoon vinegar, if wished, for this prevents the eggs whites from spreading. Put in a good pinch salt. Slide the eggs into the boiling water, leave for about 3 minutes, or until egg white is set. Insert spoon or fish slice, drain the eggs carefully and put on toast.

Scrambled eggs

1 Beat eggs, season well, and for softer mixture add 1 tablespoon milk to each 2 eggs.
2 Heat a knob of butter in pan and pour in egg mixture.
3 Cook as SLOWLY as possible, stirring all the time until lightly set.
4 Remove from heat while still a little liquid, since eggs will stiffen slightly in the pan.
5 Put on to buttered toast. Serve at once.

Variations of scrambled eggs

With chicken. Heat any tiny scraps of cooked chicken in the milk and butter, then add the beaten, seasoned eggs afterwards and cook as before.

With ham. As with chicken, but remember

ham is slightly salt, and reduce quantity of seasoning.

With prawns. As chicken, but remember all shell fish is slightly salt and reduce amount of salt with eggs.

With tomatoes. Allow 1 good sized tomato for each 2 eggs. Skin and slice thinly and heat in the butter. Beat eggs, *add no milk*, season and cook as before.

With bacon and macaroni or spaghetti. Fry the bacon in the pan—until really crisp, add the *cooked* and well drained macaroni, heat for a minute, add the eggs and cook as before.

With fried bread and onion. Chop 1 onion finely and cook in the hot butter until soft, then add a few cubes of bread and brown these. Add the beaten eggs and cook as before.

With cheese. Add a little grated Cheddar cheese to beaten eggs. Cook particularly slowly to prevent cheese becoming 'stringy'.

Looking after your omelette pan

1 An omelette pan is very precious because it makes all the difference to the success of cooking your omelettes.
   If possible buy a special pan and keep it just for omelettes or omelettes and pancakes.
2 Don't wash it, but when you have finished using it, clean it with very soft paper (modern soft kitchen rolls are ideal for this) and put it away.
3 Never get the butter so hot that there is a possibility of anything burning in this pan.
4 If you treat your pan well you should get years of wear from it.

Omelettes

1 Allow 1½–2 eggs per person.
2 Beat in a basin. (Don't forget to break them separately into a cup, in case one should be bad, before transferring them to the basin.)
3 Add a good pinch of salt and pepper, and for each 2 eggs a tablespoon of water.
4 Put a knob of butter into smallest pan.
5 When hot pour in the eggs.
6 Leave for about a minute over a high heat, when the bottom will have set.
7 Loosen the egg mixture from the sides of the pan and cook rapidly, tipping the pan from side to side, so that the liquid egg flows underneath and cooks quickly.
8 When the egg is as set as you like it, for taste varies, slip your palette knife under the omelette and fold it away from the handle.
9 Grasp the handle firmly and tip on to a hot plate or dish.
10 Garnish with parsley.
11 Serve immediately as omelettes must be eaten as soon as they are cooked.
12 *Note:* Do not cook more than 4 eggs in a 6-inch pan, otherwise cooking will take too long and the omelette will become dry.

Fillings for omelettes

Mixed herb omelette
Add finely chopped herbs to your beaten eggs.
Cheese omelette
Grated cheese should be either mixed with the eggs or better still put over the eggs just before they are set and folded.
Macaroni omelette
2 oz. cooked macaroni mixed with 3 eggs. Just before folding put grated cheese through the middle.
Ham omelette
Either mix finely diced ham with the eggs or put ham in a creamy sauce through the middle as a filling.
Chicken omelette
Either mix finely diced chicken with the eggs or put chicken in a creamy sauce through the middle as a filling.
Mushroom omelette
Cook mushrooms and mix with the eggs, or put through the middle in a creamy sauce.
Tomato omelette
Simmer tomatoes in butter or margarine until tender, season well, and use as a filling.

To fry or grill mushrooms

Mushrooms are not only an excellent accompaniment to so many dishes, but can in themselves form a savoury dish. Either grill or fry and serve on hot buttered toast. Use plenty of butter or fat to keep mushrooms moist.

Fish cakes

cooking time   6–8 minutes

you will need:

8 oz. mashed potato	1 egg
8 oz. cooked fish	flour
1 egg or 1 gill thick	crisp breadcrumbs
white sauce (see	fat for frying
page 90)	salt and pepper

1 Mix the potatoes and cooked flaked fish (cod, hake or other white fish) thoroughly with a fork.
2 Add the beaten egg or sauce, salt and pepper. Form into about 8 flat cakes.
3 Roll these cakes in a little flour, then brush lightly with beaten egg and coat with breadcrumbs.
4 Heat the fat in the frying pan and when a

faint haze is seen fry quickly on one side, turn and fry again on the other side.

5 Drain on crumpled tissue paper or kitchen roll for about 2 minutes and serve at once.

Fish croquettes

Follow directions for fish cakes, but use the white sauce, not the egg and 1 teacup breadcrumbs instead of mashed potato.

Smoked finnan haddock

cooking time   5–12 minutes

Method 1. Cut off the side fins and tail of the fish, then divide into the required number of portions. Put water into a saucepan and when boiling put in the fish. Cook steadily for about 5 minutes. Strain well with a fish slice and put on to hot plates. Put a good knob of margarine on top before serving. Don't salt the water since smoked fish has a 'salty' flavour.

Method 2. Put pieces of fish into a baking dish and half cover with milk. Put a margarined paper on top of the dish and bake in a moderately hot oven (400°F.—Gas Mark 5) for 10–12 minutes. Top with a fried egg if desired.

Herrings

cooking time   8–20 minutes

Herrings are an excellent breakfast meal and can be cooked in a variety of ways.

1 **To fry.** Put a very little fat in the frying pan, in fact some people just put a little salt in and cook the herrings without any fat at all. Cook steadily on both sides until just tender.
See also herring recipes (pages 19 to 20).

2 **To grill.** Season and brush with a little melted margarine.
Cook under a hot grill to brown both sides then lower the heat to cook through to the centre.

3 **To bake.** Put into a dish with seasoning and a squeeze of lemon juice and a little margarine. Bake in a moderately hot oven (400°F.—Gas Mark 5) for approximately 20 minutes.

Kippers

cooking time   approximately 5 minutes

Allow 1 large or 2 small kippers per person.

Cut off the heads, then wash and dry. Either cook under the grill, fry, or cook in hot water. The first method will appeal to those who like their kippers crisp, the last to those who like them soft and rather underdone.

1 **To grill.** Heat the grill, put the fish on the rack with a small knob of margarine on each fish. Cook rapidly for about 5 minutes. You need not turn the fish.

2 **To fry.** Heat a little margarine in the frying pan and fry the fish on the underside first for about 5 minutes. Turn and cook for the same time.
With both grilling and frying serve on hot plates with any liquid left from cooking poured over.

3 **In hot water.** Stand the kippers in a large jug, then pour over boiling water. Leave for about 5 minutes. Drain, put on to hot plates and put a knob of margarine on top. Or drain and put under a hot grill for 1 minute.

Bloaters

cooking time   approximately 10 minutes

These can be cooked in just the same way as kippers except that being thicker (as they are not split open) they take a little longer. The boiling water method can also be used and the bloaters then covered with a little margarine and put under a hot grill for about 4 minutes.

To make good toast

1 Before cutting the bread make sure the grill is hot.

2 Put the bread on the grid in the grill pan and hold it under the grill until brown.

3 Turn over and do the same the other side.

4 When the toast is cooked don't lay it flat on plates or the kitchen table, for the hot toast causes moisture to form and makes it limp and soggy. Give the toast a good bang on each side to let the steam out, then stand it up at once in a toast rack. If you have no rack, then support it against the back of the cooker until cold.

5 Try not to make the toast too soon before breakfast, for it spoils with long waiting. If you have an electric toaster, follow directions for particular make.

Mid-morning Drinks

It is a very good idea for a busy housewife to make a point of stopping in the middle of the morning and having just a few minutes break with a drink and perhaps a biscuit or small cake. Variety will add to your enjoyment, so don't always make yourself tea or coffee, but occasionally try something new, such as a cup of hot chocolate or a refreshing glass of lemonade. To make lemonade, use 2 lemons to a pint of boiling water. Grate the rind, being careful to use only the lemon 'zest'. Put into a jug and pour over boiling water. Add the juice and sugar to taste and leave until cold and strain. A milk shake can also be very delicious, particularly in the summer time. Put the milk, a spoonful of ice cream if desired, and whatever flavouring you choose into either an electric blender or a bowl and whisk until light and fluffy. Children should also be encouraged to have a mid-morning drink of milk, to set the pattern they observe when they go to school.

Chapter 3

Main Meal—Soups

A good nourishing home-made soup makes an excellent beginning to the main meal and some easy and favourite ones are included in this section.
If you are buying some of the first rate canned soups available you can add extra nourishment by putting in milk, cream or butter or an extra flavour by adding herbs.

Chicken soup

cooking time   1½ hours approximately

you will need:

bones of 1 chicken	1 oz. butter
5 oz. cooked chicken meat	1 tablespoon cornflour
½ pint milk	2 pints chicken stock

*You will obtain this chicken stock from boiling a chicken, but if you have roasted the chicken it is suggested you use a chicken bouillon cube dissolved in water.

1 Simmer the carcase in the stock for 1 hour, then strain. Add the cooked chicken meat and milk and cook for a further 15 minutes, then rub through sieve.
2 Blend with cornflour, add butter, seasoning. Cook for 10 minutes.

Cauliflower soup

cooking time   35 minutes

you will need:

1 large cauliflower	1 small onion
2 oz. butter	seasoning
yolk of 1 hard-boiled egg	½ gill milk or cream from top of milk
1 large potato	paprika pepper
1½ pints water	

1 Cut the cauliflower into small pieces, use a fair amount of the stalk.
2 Put into a saucepan with the onion, diced potato and 1½ pints boiling water.
3 Simmer gently for 15 minutes then remove several of the best shaped flowerets of cauliflower.
4 Continue cooking for a further 20 minutes, adding seasoning to taste.
5 Put the soup through a sieve, return to the saucepan together with the butter and cream and cook gently for a further 5 minutes.
6 Garnish with the small flowerets, sieved egg yolk and paprika pepper.

Consommé

cooking time   1 hour

you will need:

12 oz. shin of beef	1 carrot
2 pints good stock	small piece celery
seasoning	sprig parsley
1 onion	bay leaf

1 Cut the meat into small pieces.

2 Put into the saucepan with the other ingredients.
3 Simmer very gently for 1 hour.
4 Strain through several thicknesses of muslin.
5 Add 1 dessertspoon sherry if desired.
6 To clear a consommé put in a stiffly beaten egg white and clean egg shell.
7 Gently simmer again for 20 minutes, then re-strain.

The garnish gives the title to the consommé:

Consommé Julienne is a clear soup garnished with cooked 'matchsticks' of mixed vegetables.
Consomméé au vermicelli. Cook a small quantity of vermicelli in the consommé.

Cold consommé

cooking time	1 hour

1 Make consommé (see page 13) and allow to cool, when it will set into a light jelly.
2 If the weather is hot and you have no refrigerator, dissolve 2 *level* teaspoons powdered gelatine in the consommé.
3 Beat lightly before putting into soup cups.
4 Garnish with slices of cucumber or lemon or smoked salmon.

Lentil soup

cooking time	1½ hours

you will need:

8 oz. washed lentils	½ oz. flour
1 pint stock or water	1 oz. butter
little chopped bacon	½ pint milk
1 onion	little chopped thyme
1 carrot	or parsley
seasoning	

1 Put the lentils, bacon, chopped onion, carrot and stock into a pan.
2 Add seasoning and thyme and simmer gently for about 1¼ hours. Sieve.
3 The lentils can be soaked overnight if wished.
4 Add the seasoning at the very beginning of cooking.
5 Meanwhile make a very thin sauce with the butter, flour and milk.
6 Add the lentil purée and re-heat.
7 Season to taste.
8 Garnish with chopped parsley.

Variations

Lentil and celery soup
Use about 6 oz. lentils and 4 oz. chopped celery.
Lentil and tomato soup
Use 4 oz. lentils only and 8 oz. tomatoes.

Minestrone soup

cooking time	approximately 2 hours

you will need:

3 oz. haricot beans	1 dessertspoon chopped parsley
piece chopped celery	
seasoning	1 tablespoon grated onion
2 oz. quick-cooking macaroni	8 oz. tomatoes
	8 oz. chopped cabbage
1 oz. dripping or oil	1 oz. grated cheese
water	(Parmesan if possible)

1 Soak the beans for 24 hours then simmer in about 1½ pints water or stock until soft.
2 Boil macaroni for 5 minutes in 1 pint of boiling water.
3 Heat dripping, fry the onions, celery and parsley for five minutes.
4 Add chopped tomatoes, cabbage and 1 pint water and bring to the boil.
5 Put in the beans, macaroni and seasoning.
6 Simmer for 20 minutes.
7 Serve sprinkled with grated cheese.
This soup is very thick.

Cream of mushroom soup

cooking time	15–20 minutes

you will need:

8 oz. mushrooms	1 pint milk or milk and chicken stock
dash of vinegar	
few bacon rinds	seasoning
2 oz. butter	2 tablespoons cream or top of the milk
1 oz. cornflour	
	grated nutmeg

1 Wash mushrooms, but leave them whole.
2 Put them with 1 pint water, a dash of vinegar and bacon rinds into a pan, bring slowly to the boil, then simmer till tender, about 10 minutes.
3 Strain water and reserve, discard rinds and cut mushrooms into strips.
4 Melt butter in the pan, add cornflour and mix well, then add the milk, stir until boiling and cook for a few minutes.
5 Stir in the mushrooms and the water in which they were cooked, bring to boiling point again, season carefully, stir in the cream just before serving and add a grating of nutmeg.
6 Garnish with croûtons of fried bread.

Onion soup

cooking time	30 minutes

you will need:

1½ lb. onions	2 pints stock
1 oz. butter	seasoning
grated cheese	4 slices toast

1 Melt the fat in the bottom of a saucepan.
2 Slice the onions thinly and fry in the hot fat until a very pale golden brown.
3 Add the liquid and seasoning.
4 Bring slowly to the boil, lower heat and simmer gently for 30 minutes.
5 Put each slice of hot buttered toast on a soup plate.
6 Pour over the soup and sprinkle cheese on top.

Dried pea soup

cooking time   1½ hours

you will need:

8 oz. dried peas	1 teaspoon sugar
2 pints bacon stock*	sprig mint
2 onions	seasoning
1 carrot	2 rashers bacon
1 turnip	

*When you have stock left from boiling a piece of bacon, try to use it in a soup like this, because the flavour is excellent. A lentil soup or vegetable soup can be made with bacon stock too with very good results.

1 Soak the peas overnight in the bacon stock, put into saucepan with the vegetables, seasoning and mint and simmer gently for approximately 1¼–1½ hours.
2 Either rub through a sieve or beat until very smooth.
3 Taste and re-season.
4 Garnish with crisp pieces of bacon.

Creamed spinach soup

cooking time   20 minutes

you will need:

1 lb. spinach or 1 small packet frozen spinach	1 oz. cornflour
	1½ pints milk
1 oz. butter	2 egg yolks
1 small onion—sliced	3 tablespoons cream
salt	nutmeg
pepper	

1 Cook and sieve the spinach.
2 Heat the butter in a saucepan and sauté the onion until tender, but not brown.
3 Add the cornflour, mix well and cook for a few minutes.
4 Add the milk, stir till boiling and boil for 3 minutes. Strain the sauce on to the spinach, then return to the heat.
5 Mix the egg yolks and cream, add a little of the soup, then return all to the saucepan.
6 Add seasonings and reheat gently before serving, for several minutes.
7 *Do not allow to boil.*
8 Garnish with croûtons of fried bread.

Clear tomato soup

cooking time   25 minutes

you will need:

1½ lb. tomatoes	1 pint water or white stock
small piece celery	
1 small chopped onion	½ small beetroot (preferably uncooked)
few drops Worcester- shire sauce	
	1 teaspoon vinegar or lemon juice
seasoning	
2 bay leaves	

1 Put ingredients all together in a large saucepan and cook gently until the tomatoes are very soft.

2 This should take about 25 minutes.
3 Remove the beetroot and bay leaves, then rub first through a sieve and finally strain through muslin.
4 Reheat.

Cream of tomato soup

cooking time   1¼ hours

you will need:

1 lb. tomatoes	a bouquet garni
1 onion	salt
1 carrot	pepper
1 stick celery	¾ oz. cornflour
little fat bacon	¼–½ pint milk
1½ pints stock	pinch sugar

1 Slice the vegetables.
2 Fry the bacon slowly to extract the fat, then add the vegetables and sauté for about 10 minutes.
3 Add the stock (or water), seasoning and *bouquet garni,* bring to the boil and simmer gently until tender (about 1 hour).
4 Remove the *bouquet garni*, rub the soup through a fine sieve, and add the cornflour, blended with milk.
5 Return to the pan, bring just to the boil, stirring well, and cook gently for 2–3 minutes.
6 Re-season, add the sugar and serve with your chosen garnish (parsley, tiny fried croûtons of bread).

Quick vegetable soup

cooking time   8–10 minutes

you will need:

approximately 1¼ lb. mixed vegetables	1½ pints stock or water with bouillon cube
chopped parsley	grated cheese
seasoning	

1 Peel and grate the vegetables on a coarse grater.
2 Bring the stock or water and bouillon cube to the boil, add the vegetables and seasoning and cook rapidly for about 5–8 minutes until the vegetables are just tender.
3 Pour into hot soup cups and sprinkle with lots of grated cheese and parsley.
4 Do choose a good mixture of vegetables for an interesting flavour.

Vegetable broth

cooking time   approximately 30 minutes

you will need:

1¼ lb. mixed vegetables	seasoning
	1 oz. rice or pearl barley
chopped parsley	1½ pints stock or water
grated cheese	with a bouillon cube

1 Peel and cut the vegetables into small dice or grate them very coarsely.
2 If using pearl barley blanch this by putting

into cold water, bringing to the boil and cooking for 1 minute.
Strain, then cook in boiling salted water until tender.
If using rice cook in boiling salted water until soft.

5 Meanwhile put the vegetables and stock into pan and cook until tender; .his will vary according to how large the pieces are but will take from 10–20 minutes.
6 Add the barley or rice and re-heat then serve garnished with chopped parsley and cheese.

Chapter 4

Main Meal—Fish

In the following chapter you will find a chart on the best ways to cook familiar fish and also some less usual recipes. The haddock recipes have been chosen to give you ideas for economical white fish, but in place of haddock you can use cod, hake or huss.
The herring recipes could be made with trout or mackerel and the quick sole recipe (see page 21) will suggest, I hope, ways of producing a gourmet's dish without spending too much time.

Fish Buying Guide

name	type	in season	best cooked by
Bream	White	July–December	Baking or grilling.
Carp	Freshwater	October–February	Grilling, frying when young, baking when older.
Cod	White	Throughout the year: best October–March	All methods. Excellent in 'made-up' dishes.
Crab	Shell fish	May–August	Dressing and serving cold.
Dog fish or huss	White	September–May	Baking or frying.
Dory or John Dory	White	September–early January	Same method as for sole or turbot.
Eel	Freshwater	September–May	Stewing or making into jelly.
Eel	Smoked	Throughout year	Serving as an hors-d'oeuvre with horseradish sauce, lemon and brown bread and butter.
Flounder	White	November–March	Same method as for plaice or sole.
Haddock	White	October–February	Same method as for cod.
Haddock	Smoked	Throughout year	Poaching or as kedgeree.
Hake	White	June–January	Frying or baking.
Halibut	White	July–April	Poaching, grilling or baking; if under 3 lb. should be baked whole.
Herrings	Oily	Throughout year from various sources. British season June–February	Grilling, baking, frying or pickling and sousing with salads.

name	type	in season	best cooked by
Herring	Smoked	Throughout year	Bloaters—grilling or frying. Buckling—same method as for smoked trout. Kippers—frying, grilling, baking, boiling.
Huss (see dogfish)			
John Dory (see Dory)			
Lobster	Shellfish	February–October	Cold in salads. Heated in sauce.
Mackerel	Oily	March–July	Same methods as herrings.
Mullet	Oily	April–October	Baking or grilling.
Oysters	Shellfish	September–April	On shell—uncooked or fried.
Perch	Freshwater	May–February	Frying or poaching.
Plaice	White	Late May–December	Baking, frying, grilling. Steaming or poaching for invalids.
Prawns	Shellfish	Small: February–October Large: March–December	Serving hot or cold in main dish or with sauce.
Salmon	Oily	March–August	Serving hot or cold.
Salmon	Smoked	Throughout year	Not cooked. Served as hors-d'oeuvre or in sandwiches.
Salmon trout	Oily	April–August	Same method as salmon.
Shrimps	Shellfish	February–October	Same method as prawns.
Skate	White	November–May	Frying, baking or poaching. Use cold in salads.
Sole	White	Some kind available all year	Baking, frying, poaching, steaming, grilling and serving either with lemon and melted butter, or other sauces.
Sprats	Oily	October–March	Baked or fried.
Sprats	Smoked	Throughout year	Grilling or frying.
Trout	Smoked	Throughout year	Serving as an hors-d'oeuvre as smoked eel.
Trout	Freshwater	April–September	Grilling, frying, baking.
Turbot	White	April–early September	Baking, grilling, frying, poaching or serving cold in fish salads.
Whitebait	Oily	May–August	Frying in deep fat.
Whiting	White	October–April	Poaching, baking, grilling, frying.
Whiting	Smoked (golden fillets)	Throughout year	Same method as smoked haddock.

How to tell if fish is fresh

1 Stale fish is not only most unpleasant but quite a dangerous food to serve.
2 The way one tells if fish is fresh is if it is firm, pleasant smelling and the eyes and scales look bright.
3 With shell fish it is fresh if a bright colour, in the case of lobsters and prawns if the tails spring back after being pulled out. It is of good quality if it feels weighty for the size, poor quality shell fish feels light because it is full of water.
4 Whilst you can buy many fish throughout the year the fish buying guide does give you the best times to have them.

Baked fish

Most fish can be baked, but care should be taken with fillets of fish to keep them moist.
1 Butter the dish well.
2 Put in fish and season.
3 Add a little stock, milk or white wine to keep fish moist. (Use this stock in sauces.)
4 Cover with buttered paper.
5 Place in a moderate to moderately hot oven (375–400°F.—Gas Mark 4–5).
6 Bake fillets of plaice, sole, etc. for approximately 12–20 minutes.
7 Bake cutlets of white fish for approximately 20 minutes.
8 Bake whole fish for approximately 12 minutes per lb. (if stuffed weigh with stuffing).

To poach fish

1 Salt water and bring to a gentle boil. Or prepare fish stock by adding bones and skin of fish plus a bay leaf, onion or carrot. Bring to the boil.
2 Lower fish gently into simmering water. Never boil fish rapidly. It is inclined to break and will certainly become very dry.
3 Poach until cooked.
4 Allow 7 minutes per lb. for thin fillets of fish, and 10 minutes per lb. for thick cutlets.
5 If poaching in 1 piece then allow 12 minutes first lb. and 10 minutes after that for second lb.
6 For a very large fish allow 7–8 minutes per lb. for any weight after first 2 lb.

Crisp-topped haddock

cooking time   20–25 minutes

you will need:

1 lb. fillet of haddock	6 level tablespoons
salt	fresh white breadcrumbs
pepper	1 oz. margarine
3 tablespoons milk	

1 level tablespoon	1 level tablespoon
chopped onion	chopped parsley
2 oz. mushrooms,	2 tomatoes
chopped	

1 Cut the fillet into convenient serving portions and arrange in a greased ovenproof dish.
2 Season well.
3 Sauté the onions and mushrooms in the margarine, add the remaining ingredients except tomatoes and mix well.
4 Spread over the fish and arrange halved tomatoes in between the portions.
5 Bake in a moderate oven (375°F.—Gas Mark 4) for 20 minutes.

Fish in savoury custard

cooking time   1 hour

you will need:

12 oz. white fish	2 eggs (or egg yolks)
½ pint milk	little chopped parsley
seasoning	and/or grated onion
pinch thyme	lemon and parsley to
little butter	garnish

1 Butter a dish and put in the fish, season.
2 Beat eggs well, add milk, seasoning and flavourings.
3 Pour over fish and bake in a slow oven (275–300°F.—Gas Mark 2) for about 1 hour.
4 Garnish with lemon and parsley.
5 To make a change, serve it au gratin. Top with crumbs and grated cheese.

Fish hash

cooking time   10 minutes

you will need:

12 oz. cooked white fish	12 oz. mashed potatoes
little chopped parsley	seasoning
grated lemon rind	fat for frying
beetroot to garnish	little milk if necessary

1 Mix fish, potatoes and flavourings well.
2 If stiff add a very little milk.
3 Heat a knob of fat in pan and cook the mixture steadily until very hot and golden brown.
4 Fold like an omelette and serve with sliced beetroot.

Fish mixed grill

1 Take a selection of fish foods such as white fish either filleted or cut into neat fingers. Cod, fresh haddock, whiting are ideal. OR sardine, prawns, herrings and/or herring roes.
2 Allow a small portion of each per person.
3 Cook under a hot grill, brushing with PLENTY of melted butter.
4 Serve on a large platter.
5 Garnish with parsley and grilled tomatoes.

Fried fish

This is one of the most popular ways of serving any fish. It is important to remember the following:

1 Dry the fish well and coat very thinly with seasoned flour.
2 Dip in fritter batter or in beaten egg and crumbs. Shake off surplus crumbs or allow excess batter to drain away.
3 For shallow frying make sure the fat (which can be oil, cooking fat, butter) is hot. Put in the fish, cook steadily until brown, turn and cook on the other side. If using deep fat make sure this is not too hot otherwise the outside browns before the fish is cooked.
4 Always drain fried fish. Use kitchen paper. The latest absorbent kitchen rolls are excellent, but never greaseproof paper.
5 Do not overcook the fish.
6 For shallow frying allow 2–3 minutes on either side for filleted fish, 4–5 minutes for thicker fish cutlets or whole fish.
7 For deep frying allow 3–4 minutes total cooking time for fillets, 7–8 minutes for whole fish or cutlets.

Grilled fish

Most fish is suitable for grilling.
1 Make sure that the grill is hot before you begin cooking.
2 Keep the fish well brushed with melted butter so that it doesn't dry.
3 Most fillets can be grilled without turning. Allow approximately 4 minutes, turning the heat down after the first 2–3 minutes if desired.
4 If fillets are very thick they must be turned. Grill quickly for 2–3 minutes on either side then reduce heat for a further 3–4 minutes.
5 Grilled mushrooms which can be cooked at the same time are an ideal accompaniment for any grilled fish.

Haddock au gratin

cooking time · · · · · · · · · · · · 15–20 minutes

you will need:

1 good-sized smoked haddock or haddock fillet	2 hard-boiled eggs (if wished)
6 oz. grated cheese	1 small onion
1½ oz. flour	2 large tomatoes
2 oz. butter	½ pint milk
	seasoning

1 Put the haddock into the milk with a little seasoning and cook until just tender.
2 Drain and flake the fish, and strain off the milk.
3 Fry the chopped onion in the butter.

4 Add the flour and cook gently for several minutes.
5 Add the milk left from cooking the fish.
6 Bring the sauce to the boil and cook until thickened.
7 Season well, add the fish, chopped eggs and nearly all the cheese.
8 Pile into a hot dish.
9 Cover with the rest of the cheese and the thinly sliced tomatoes and cook for a further 10 minutes in the oven or about 5 minutes under a hot grill. Serve at once.

Haddock casserole

cooking time · · · · · · · · · · · · 20 minutes

you will need:

1¼ lb. fresh haddock fillet, skinned

for the sauce

2 oz. margarine	3 sticks celery, chopped
1 oz. flour	8 oz. tomatoes, skinned,
1 gill stock	quartered and seeded
1 dessertspoon tomato	pinch of thyme
purée	salt and pepper
1 large onion, sliced	

1 Melt the margarine and cook the onion and celery until soft but not coloured.
2 Add the flour and cook for 2–3 minutes.
3 Stir in the remaining ingredients, bring slowly to the boil and simmer for 3–4 minutes, stirring continuously.
4 Cut the haddock into portions and arrange in an ovenproof dish.
5 Pour the sauce over and bake in a moderate oven (375°F.—Gas Mark 5) for 20 minutes.

Baked herrings

cooking time · · · · · · · · · · · · 30 minutes

To preserve the full flavour, try herrings cooked in paper bags.
1 Butter each fish well, season and flavour with a little lemon juice.
2 Put into a greaseproof paper bag, seal edges tightly.
3 Bake for about 30 minutes in a moderately hot oven (350°F.—Gas Mark 4).
4 Do not remove from bags until ready to serve.

Herring pie

cooking time · · · · · · · · · · · · 30 minutes

you will need:

pepper	
4 good-sized herrings	1 oz. butter
4 good-sized potatoes	1 large cooking apple
salt	sliced beetroot

1 Bone and fillet the herrings and put on to a dish, sprinkling them with salt and pepper.
2 Butter the sides of a pie dish well and line with thinly sliced potatoes, season well.

3 Arrange the herrings and sliced apples in the centre of the dish.
4 Cover with a layer of sliced potatoes.
5 Season well and cover with buttered paper.
6 Bake for approximately 30 minutes in a moderately hot oven (400°F.—Gas Mark 5).
7 Remove the paper and cook for a further 20 or 25 minutes until the potatoes are tender and golden brown.
8 Serve with sliced beetroot.

Grilled herrings in oatmeal

cooking time   10–12 minutes

you will need:

4 herrings	good pinch salt and
2 tomatoes	pepper
parsley	1 oz. margarine
2 tablespoons medium-	a little beaten egg
ground oatmeal	

1 Halve the tomatoes, put into the grill pan, with a sprinkling of salt and pepper and little margarine on top.
2 Mix a good pinch salt and pepper with oatmeal.
3 Prepare the herrings, making 3 slits on top with a sharp knife to prevent the skin from curling badly.
4 Coat herrings thinly with beaten egg.
5 Roll the herrings thickly in the oatmeal.
6 Put on the grid over the tomatoes, and under the hot grill.
7 Cook quickly for about 4 minutes, turn, then cook for the same length of time on the under side, basting with fat from the pan.
8 Reduce heat and cook steadily for a further 3–4 minutes.
9 Garnish with the tomatoes and parsley.

Herrings meunière

cooking time   10 minutes

you will need:

4 large herrings	juice of ½ lemon
seasoning	chopped parsley
2 oz. butter	1 teaspoon finely chopped
few capers	onion
lemon	watercress
little flour	

1 Clean herrings.
2 Take out roes, remove heads and backbones.
3 Roll in seasoned flour.
4 Heat butter in pan, add herrings and fry steadily.
5 Put roes in during cooking.
6 When cooked remove fish to hot dish.
7 Add juice of lemon, parsley and capers and onion to the butter and cook butter until dark brown.

8 Pour over fish.
9 Garnish with wedges of lemon and watercress.
10 To make a change, when the fish are nearly cooked add 2 or 3 tablespoons cream and the onion, capers etc. Cook until fish are quite tender, basting with cream mixture.

Kedgeree

cooking time   10 minutes plus rice cooking time

you will need:

6 oz. cooked smoked	pinch cayenne pepper
haddock	and salt
1 hard-boiled egg	chopped parsley
approximately 8 oz.	lemon quarters
cooked rice	

1 Flake fish coarsely with a fork.
2 Chop the egg white, sieve the yolk and put on one side for garnishing.
3 Mix the flaked fish, chopped egg white, cooked rice and seasoning in a saucepan over moderate heat until hot, with a fork, adding little milk if necessary.
4 Pile the mixture into a hot entrée dish, garnish with chopped parsley and sieved egg yolk and serve at once with lemon quarters.

Grilled mackerel

cooking time   approximately 12 minutes

you will need:

4 mackerel	pepper
1 oz. margarine	lemon
salt	parsley

1 Cut the heads off the mackerel and remove bones.
2 Heat the grill.
3 Fold the mackerel over again after you have taken out the bones.
4 Put the fish on the grill grid.
5 Put a small knob of margarine on each.
6 Sprinkle with salt and pepper.
7 Cook rapidly for about 4 minutes.
8 Turn the fish, put a little more margarine on top and seasoning and cook for a further 4 minutes.
9 Lower the heat of the grill to give a further 2 or 3 minutes cooking.
10 These are solid fish and therefore take rather a long time to cook. Serve on hot dish with any margarine that has dropped into the grill pan poured over. Garnish with rings of lemon and sprigs of parsley.
11 Grilled mackerel is also good with gooseberry sauce, made as follows: Simmer fruit in water until tender, sieve, return to pan and reheat with sugar to taste and a small knob of margarine or butter.

Plaice whirls

cooking time   15 minutes

you will need:

8 small fillets of plaice	2 oz. shrimps or prawns
3 oz. breadcrumbs	1 oz. butter or margarine
seasoning	little chopped parsley

for the sauce

1 oz. butter	1 oz. flour
½ pint milk	few drops anchovy essence

1 Chop the prawns and mix with the crumbs, parsley, half the butter and the seasoning.
2 Spread this mixture on to the fillets of fish and roll tightly.
3 Put into a dish and cover with buttered paper after moistening the fish with just a little milk.
4 Bake for approximately 15 minutes in moderately hot oven.
5 Meanwhile prepare the sauce, add any liquid from the fish to the sauce.
6 Coat the fish with the sauce and serve.

Sole in mushroom sauce

cooking time   25 minutes

you will need:

4 large fillets of sole or plaice	1 can condensed cream of mushroom soup
salt	1 tablespoon milk
pepper	sherry to taste (optional)
juice ½ lemon	

1 Wash and trim fillets.
2 Sprinkle with seasoning and lemon juice and roll from head to tail.
3 Place in a greased ovenproof dish.
4 Put the condensed cream of mushroom soup into a basin, beat in the milk, sherry and a teaspoon of lemon juice.
5 Pour over the fish, cover with a greased paper and bake in a moderate oven (375°F.—Gas Mark 4) for 20–25 minutes.
6 Serve at once.

Chapter 5

Main Meal—Meat

Meat is one of the major foods bought in most households and since its price is high, it is worth while using it in the wisest possible way. Remember that it does pay you to buy cheaper pieces of meat for they give just as much food value to the family and with careful cooking can be just as delicious.

Beef

The lean should be a clear bright red, and the fat firm and pale cream in colour. The very best joints *must* have a certain amount of fat on them.

purpose	cut to choose	cooking time	accompaniments
Roasting	Sirloin Ribs Fillet Aitch-bone (good quality) Topside Rump	15 minutes per lb. plus 15 minutes over. Well-done, 20 minutes per lb. plus 20 minutes over, or 40 minutes per lb. in very slow oven.	Mustard Horseradish sauce Yorkshire pudding Roast potatoes thin gravy
Grilling or Frying	Rump Fillet Sirloin Entrecôte	5–15 minutes per lb. depending on thickness and personal preference	Chipped or mashed potatoes Salad Tomatoes Mushrooms

purpose	cut to choose	cooking time	accompaniments
Stewing or Braising	Skirt or Chuck Bladebone 'Leg of Mutton' cut Brisket Flank Ox-tail	1½–3 hours	Mixed vegetables Dumplings Thickened gravy
Pickling or Boiling	Brisket Shin or leg Silverside Flank Aitch-bone	1½–3 hours	Vegetables or salad
Stock for Soup	Neck Shin or leg Clod Marrowbone Oxtail Flank	1½–3 hours	

Pork

The lean part of the meat must look pale pink, and the fat white and dry. Pork must never be served under-done. Try to avoid serving pork in very hot weather.

purpose	cut to choose	cooking time	accompaniments
Roasting	Loin Leg Bladebone Spare rib	25 minutes per lb. plus 25 minutes over	Sage and onion stuffing Mustard Apple sauce Orange salad
Frying or Grilling	Chops from loin Spare rib chops	15–20 minutes	Apple sauce Apple rings Sage and onion stuffing Tomatoes Mushrooms
Boiling	Head Hand and spring Belly Cuts given for roasting	2¼ hours	Salads Mixed vegetables

Mutton or Lamb

See that the lean is dull red, but very firm. The fat should be white in colour. You can differentiate between lamb and mutton—lamb is paler in colour. But in many recipes either can be used. Mutton naturally needs longer cooking time in stewing.

purpose	cut to choose	cooking time	accompaniments
Roasting	Leg Loin and Saddle Best end of Neck (lamb) Shoulder Breast, stuffed and rolled	20 minutes per lb. plus 20 minutes over	Mutton, redcurrant jelly Lamb, mint sauce Fresh peas
Grilling or Frying	Loin chops Gigot chops Cutlets	10–15 minutes	Chipped potatoes Tomatoes, mushrooms, peas, salads
Stewing Braising or Boiling	Neck Breast Leg Shoulder	$1\frac{1}{2}$–$2\frac{1}{2}$ hours	Mixed vegetables Creamed potatoes
Soups or Stock	Scrag end of neck Head Trotter	$1\frac{1}{2}$–$2\frac{1}{2}$ hours	

Veal

Be very critical, particularly in hot weather, as veal does not keep well. There is little fat to see, but what there is should be firm and white, the lean must look dry and be a pale pink.

purpose	cut to choose	cooking time	accompaniments
Roasting	Shoulder Breast Best end of neck Loin Fillet Chump end of loin	25 minutes per lb. plus 25 minutes over	Sausages Veal stuffing or other well flavoured stuffing Keep well basted
Grilling or Frying	Chops from loin Fillet Best end of neck chops Thin slices from leg	15–20 minutes 5–6 minutes	Chipped potatoes Tomatoes Mushrooms
Stewing or Braising	Breast Fillet Knuckle Middle and scrag end of neck	$1\frac{1}{2}$–$2\frac{1}{2}$ hours	Mixed vegetables Various sauces

purpose	cut to choose	cooking time	accompaniments
Boiling	Head Feet Breast	1½–2½ hours	Mixed vegetables or salads
Stock for soups	Feet Knuckle	1½–2½ hours	

Offal buying guide

name	to cook
BRAINS	The brains from calves', pigs' or sheeps' head can be served in a thick sauce on toast or as a sauce. They are very nutritious.
FEET	The feet of calf and pig contain a great deal of gelatine and are used to help set moulds and brawn.
HEAD	The head of a calf is considered the most delicate in flavour but both sheeps' and pigs' heads can be used in exactly the same way. A recipe is given for preparing calf's head (see page 31), also brawn (see page 31).
HEART	The small heart of sheep, calf or pig can be stuffed and roasted. Ox heart is inclined to be tough and can be casseroled slowly in thick brown sauce. Halve the heart, fill with sage and onion stuffing (see page 91), wrap in buttered foil and roast for 1¼ hours in a moderately hot oven (400°F.—Gas Mark 5).
KIDNEYS	These can be used in a number of ways as a savoury dish by themselves, fried with bacon, served on toast as a savoury. The kidneys from pig, calf or lamb are all very tender and can be cooked fairly quickly. All that is needed is to remove the gristle and skin and toss in seasoned flour and fry in butter for 10 minutes. Ox kidney, on the other hand, is much tougher and should be used in recipes with prolonged cooking.
LIVER	This is a very important food and is a rich source of food values particularly for young children and invalids. Calves' liver has the highest quality. Liver gets tough by over-cooking. Fry or grill for 6–7 minutes only using plenty of fat.
TAIL	It is the tail of an ox which is used in cooking and this provides a first class meal (see page 35).
TONGUE	Small tongue from calf, sheep or pig can be used in exactly the same way as ox tongue. Recipes are given for cooking and pressing these (see page 36), but the tongue when once boiled and skinned can be heated in a brown or Madeira sauce and served with vegetables as a hot meal.
TRIPE	Whilst many people dislike this intensely it is a first class food at a very economical price. It comes from the stomach of the animal (see page 39).

To carve meat

Good carving takes practice, but there are certain rules to help you.

1 Do buy a good knife—and if you have a large family or entertain a great deal, it is wise to have 2 knives, since the heat of the meat when cooked is inclined to blunt the knife.

2 To carve beef—cut long slices across the joint. When carving sirloin on the bone you must, however, first, remove the top bone or chine, cut the first slices along the bone, then turn the joint and cut thick slices at right angles from the bone.

3 To carve lamb or mutton—cut rather thicker slices downwards. The shoulder is not easy to carve, but you should follow the formation of the bone, which means carving round it, starting in the centre of the joint and cutting diagonal slices.

4 To carve pork—cut downwards as for mutton. Ask the butcher to chine, i.e. cut through bones, on loin.

5 To carve veal—most joints as beef, but shoulder as for mutton, loin as for pork.

6 To carve joints of bacon—since bacon has been boned, generally cut across. A whole ham on the bone should be carved diagonally, the first cuts when the ham is large should be downwards.

To fry meat

Do not have the fat too hot in the pan before adding the meat, for you do not wish to scorch the outside before the inside is tender.

1 Veal, because it has so little fat, is on the whole better fried, particularly fillets of veal, than grilled.

2 Liver should be fried for the same reason. Take particular care not to overcook liver—it needs just a few minutes. If liver is overcooked it becomes very tough and dry. Choose calves' or lamb's liver.

3 Chops of lamb, pork and mutton can be fried instead of grilled—little, if any, fat will be required.

4 Steak can be fried, but is generally considered better if grilled.

5 Bacon is considered by many people to have a better flavour if grilled, but that is just a matter of opinion.

6 Sausages should be fried steadily, and not too much fat used.

7 Kidneys need frying gently, so they do not harden on the outside.

8 Serve fried foods with 'refreshing accompaniments'—tomatoes, mushrooms, green salads.

9 For people who do not like fatty dishes, always drain on absorbent paper before serving.

10 *Electric frying pans* today mean that food can be fried on the serving table, and eaten very freshly cooked.

Times for frying meat

1 CHOPS AND CUTLETS. 3–4 minutes either side, then further 3–6 minutes on low heat.

2 STEAKS. 2–4 minutes either side. For well done steak, turn heat low and allow further 3–4 minutes. Very thin (minute) steaks take only a minute on either side, then another 2–3 minutes if well done.

3 VEAL FILLETS. 2–3 minutes on either side.

To grill meat

1 Make sure the grill is really hot before the food is put underneath; this is important since the heat of the grill seals in the flavour of the meat at once.

2 Do not try to grill meats that are not prime cut.

3 If using an infra-red grill follow the directions given by the manufacturer—the times in the meat charts are for an ordinary gas or electric grill.

Times for grilling meat under high grill

1 CHOPS. 3 minutes either side, then turn heat lower for further 3–6 minutes.

2 STEAKS. 2–4 minutes on either side under high grill, keeping well basted with hot butter. For well done steak allow further 3–4 minutes with grill turned low.

To roast meat

ROASTING is a form of cooking which must be kept for really prime joints. The following times are all for a hot oven, or at least a moderately hot oven.

1 BEEF takes 15–20 minutes per lb. according to taste, plus an additional 20 minutes.

2 MUTTON, LAMB take 20 minutes per lb. or even a little longer (since people tend to like it well done), plus an additional 20 minutes.

3 PORK, BACON, VEAL all need very good cooking, so allow 25 minutes for each lb. and 25 minutes over.

SLOW ROASTING has become very popular during the past years, and if you have any doubts as to whether the meat is tender, then choose this method.

1 Instead of roasting at from 400–450°F.—Gas

Mark 5–7, use a very slow oven (275–325°F.—Gas Mark 1–2).

2 Allow twice as long.

3 The meat will not spoil, and will certainly be more tender.

For perfect roasting

1 Do not have too much fat on the joint, otherwise you harden the outside.
BEEF needs little fat.
VEAL needs more fat. Or you can do as a French cook would and thread narrow strips of fat bacon through a large-eyed needle and push these through the veal. This produces an excellent flavour and very moist texture.
LAMB needs a little fat, if very lean, but mutton does not.
PORK does not need fat, particularly if you want to get good crackling. But you will improve the flavour of the crackling if you brush the skin with melted olive oil or butter.
BACON OR HAM should be well soaked before roasting (see page 29).

2 Covering the joint with a lid (in a covered roaster) or with foil, will not spoil it, and will keep the oven very clean. For crisp joints, particularly pork, remove the foil or lid 30 minutes before serving.

3 Do not overcook meat. It does not make it more tender, but tends to toughen it.

To make gravy for meat

Thin Gravy

It is correct to serve a thin gravy with meat that is not stuffed.

1 Pour away practically all the fat from the roasting tin, leaving the residue of meat to give flavour.

2 Add about 1 teaspoon of flour and approximately ½ pint stock, or water flavoured with meat or vegetable extract.

3 Bring to the boil.

4 Cook until clear and strain.

5 Alternatively, many people prefer just to use the natural meat juices of which there will be quite a lot if your joint is underdone.

Thick Gravy

1 Leave about 1 tablespoon of fat in the meat tin.

2 Add approximately 1 oz. flour, and cook for several minutes.

3 Add just over ½ pint stock or water flavoured with meat or vegetable extract.

4 Bring to the boil, and cook until thick.

5 Strain and serve.

To stew and braise meat

To stew meat

1 Stewing meat is a process that is done gently, so that the tough pieces of meat are made tender and kept moist during cooking.

2 Cut the meat into neat dice, not too small, or the dish will not look attractive.

3 The meat and vegetables can be tossed in fat first, but unless recipes state otherwise the meat must *not* be cooked for too long a period in the fat, otherwise it will certainly toughen.

4 Unless you are using a pressure cooker, cook very gently either in a saucepan or a casserole.

5 Allow approximately 2 hours over slow heat.

6 The mixture is generally thickened at the end of the cooking time.

To braise meat

1 Braising is the cooking term used when the meat is cooked all the time in a thick sauce or gravy.

2 Allow 2–3 hours in covered casserole in slow oven (275–300°F.—Gas Mark 2).

To make a hotpot

This is not only a very excellent way of serving stewing meat, but a labour-saving one too, since the meat and all the vegetables, including the potatoes, can be cooked and served in the same dish. All stewing pieces of beef, veal, pork or mutton and lamb are suitable. With the fatter meats, i.e. pork and mutton, it is a good idea to trim the surplus fat from the meat at the beginning and use this fat for frying lean meat and vegetables.

1 Toss meat and any vegetables—carrots, sliced onions, crushed garlic, sliced peppers etc. in a little fat then season well.

2 Put a layer of the meat and vegetable mixture, then a layer of uncooked sliced potatoes in the casserole, continue like this, seasoning each layer of potatoes well—and end with a layer of potatoes.

3 Pour over a small amount of stock.

4 Put a little fat on top of the potatoes.

5 Cover with the casserole lid or foil and cook slowly for about 2½ hours.

6 Remove the lid, so that the top layer of potatoes can become crisp and brown.

7 Serve with a green salad or green vegetables.

Using cheaper cuts of meat

LAMB

BREAST OF LAMB is delicious when stuffed and rolled, then baked or pot-roasted (see recipe on page 27).

NECK OF LAMB can be roasted if done slowly, or pot-roasted if preferred. It is much cheaper than leg or shoulder and has an excellent flavour, hot or cold. Note that it must be lamb and not mutton.

JOINTS OF LAMB OR MUTTON suitable for pot roasting are any that appear tough (e.g. imported meat sometimes tends to be tough) so be on the safe side and pot roast LEG, LOIN and SHOULDER. Always pot-roast BREAST OF MUTTON, first preparing it as stuffed breast of lamb (see page 33).

Pot roasting lamb or mutton

Heat a good knob of fat in a large saucepan. Flour and season the meat and cook in the hot fat until golden brown on the outside.

After this, use one of the following methods:

Method 1. Put a very firmly-fitting lid on the pan, turn the heat very low.

Cook, turning the meat from time to time, for about 40 minutes per lb.

You can only use this method if the pan lid DOES fit tightly and the saucepan is very strong.

An easier method is either of the following:

Method 2. Fit a trivet at the bottom of the pan.

Lift the meat on to this and add about 2–3 tablespoons water.

Put a tightly fitting lid on and cook, allowing 40 minutes per lb.

The liquid at the bottom of the pan makes delicious gravy.

Method 3. If you have no trivet, put a thick layer of well-seasoned root vegetables (whole carrots, onions, turnips) at the bottom of the pan.

Add 2–3 tablespoons of water.

Lift the meat on to the vegetables.

Do not use potatoes as they become too soft and allow the meat to drop into the liquid at the bottom of the pan.

Minced mutton

Mincing the cheaper cuts of mutton provides variation. For ways of using it, see either of the following recipes:

Mutton pudding

cooking time   2–3 hours

you will need:

8 oz. suet crust pastry (see page 64)	1 level tablespoon flour
½ teaspoon mixed herbs	1 lb. minced mutton
	1 small chopped onion
1 gill stock or water	1 oz. fat
	seasoning

1 Line the sides of a basin with the suet pastry. Leave enough over for a lid.
2 Fry the sliced onion in the hot fat, then add the flour and cook for several minutes.
3 Gradually stir in the stock.
4 Bring to the boil and cook until thickened.
5 Add the minced mutton, herbs and seasoning.
6 Cool slightly, put into the pudding.
7 Cover with suet pastry and greased paper and steam for 2 hours.

Mutton pies

cooking time   35 minutes

1 Make the filling as for the pudding, but allow only 1 gill stock or water.
2 Line deep patty tins with pastry, put in some of the mixture and a sliced hard-boiled egg if wished.
3 Cover with pastry.
4 Brush the top with milk or beaten egg.
5 Bake in the centre of a hot oven for 15 minutes.
6 Lower the heat to moderate for a further 20 minutes.

Irish stew

cooking time   just over 2 hours

you will need:

1 lb. scrag or middle neck of lamb or mutton	8 oz. onions
	1 lb. potatoes
pepper	salt
water	peas and carrots

1 Cut meat into neat pieces.
2 If using new potatoes cut 1 or 2 in halves, or if using old potatoes cut 1 large one into small slices.
3 Slice the onions.
4 Put the meat, half the pieces of potato and the sliced onions into the pan.
5 Add about ¾ pint water and plenty of salt and pepper.
6 Bring slowly to the boil, remove any scum.
7 Lower the heat and simmer gently for just over 1½ hours.
8 Add the rest of the potatoes, with a little more salt, and continue cooking for about 40 minutes.
9 To serve, pile the meat and stock in the centre of the hot dish with the potatoes round and a garnish of the freshly cooked peas and carrots.

BEEF
FLANK, FRESH BRISKET, SKIRT and cheap joints suitable for pot roasting. These can be stuffed with minced meat, sausage meat or savoury stuffings and chopped bacon, rolled, then pot roasted (see pot roasting of mutton), and make a delicious dish.

SALTED BRISKET should be soaked for several hours, then simmered gently, adding vegetables if served hot.
It is delicious cold with salad.
SILVERSIDE (a little more expensive) can be treated in the same way.
MINCED STEWING STEAK OR FLANK can be used in either of the following recipes:

Minced beef and onion mould

cooking time   2 hours

you will need:

1 lb. minced beef	2–3 oz. breadcrumbs
1 egg	pinch mixed spice
good pinch mixed herbs	1 oz. dripping
2 sliced onions	seasoning

1 Heat dripping.
2 Fry the sliced onions until soft.
3 Mix with all the other ingredients and put into a greased basin.
4 Cover with greased paper and steam for 2 hours very gently.
5 Turn out and serve with hot, thick gravy.
6 Or serve cold with salad.

Beef and cheese casserole

cooking time $1\frac{1}{4}$ hours

you will need:

8 oz. tomatoes	$\frac{1}{2}$ pint cheese sauce
8 oz. onions	(see page 90)
1 lb. minced beef	1 egg
1 lb. peeled and sliced	2 oz. margarine
potatoes	seasoning

1 Heat the margarine.
2 Fry the sliced onions and tomatoes until soft.
3 Mix with the meat, adding plenty of seasoning and a little chopped parsley if wished.
4 Put a layer of sliced and well-seasoned potatoes in the dish, then meat mixture then more potatoes. Fill the dish like this, ending with potatoes.
5 Stir the beaten egg into the cheese sauce and pour this over the meat mixture.
6 Put a lid on the dish and cook in the centre of a moderate oven (350°F.—Gas Mark 3) for about $1\frac{1}{4}$ hours.
7 Remove the lid and cook for a further 30 minutes.

Bacon

See it looks moist and not too dry, with brightly coloured lean part. Bacon may be blanched to remove excess of salt before adding to other dishes.

purpose	cut to choose	cooking time	accompaniments
Roasting or Baking	Gammon slipper Middle gammon Back and ribs Joint top streaky	20 minutes per lb. and 20 minutes over. If well done cook like pork for 25 minutes per lb.	Mustard Salads Unusual garnishes such as baked apples, oranges, pineapple, etc.
Grilling or Frying	Top streaky Prime streaky Thin streaky Gammon slipper Middle gammon Corner gammon Long back Short back Back and ribs Top back Prime collar	Few minutes only for thin rashers. With thick slices of gammon cook outside fairly quickly, then reduce heat to cook through to the middle. Keep gammon well brushed with fat when grilling.	Eggs, tomatoes, mushrooms, etc., for breakfast. Vegetables or salads for main meals.
Boiling or Braising	Forehock Prime streaky Flank Gammon slipper Gammon hock Middle gammon Corner gammon Long back Back and ribs Top back Prime collar End of collar Oyster cut	Soak well if you want very mild flavour, then simmer gently for 20-25 minutes per lb. and 20–25 minutes over. Do not boil too quickly. A pressure cooker can be used. Ham or bacon stock is excellent for soups.	Any vegetables—beans and peas are particularly good with boiled bacon. Salads, etc.

Methods of cooking bacon or ham

BACON IN THE PIECE, either hot or cold, makes a wonderful meal.

TO BOIL. The bacon should first be soaked overnight in cold water.
Then simmer very gently, allowing 20–25 minutes per lb. and 20–25 minutes over.
Do not cook too quickly.

TO BAKE. Lean cuts of bacon are suitable for cooking as joints. If fairly salt bacon, it should be soaked for several hours. Green bacon or very lightly smoked bacon needs little, if any, soaking.

HAM. The hams of the pig are simply the legs which are cut off and dry cured individually. While the various hams have their own (secret) methods of curing they are, unlike bacon, generally unsmoked. It takes from 3–5 months to cure a ham. At the end of that time a perfect ham has a faint green mould, known as the 'bloom'. Never take this off until you are ready to cook it.

Ham needs about 24 hours soaking.

GAMMON is also the leg of the pig, but it is cured with the whole bacon side before being cut away. It is, on the whole, cheaper than ham, and can be used in any recipe where ham is indicated.

Bacon and rabbit pudding

cooking time   4 hours

you will need:

8 oz. suet crust pastry
  (see page 64)

for the filling

½ large or 1 small rabbit	3 rashers bacon
¼ teaspoon salt	1 tablespoon flour
good pinch pepper	good pinch sage
¾ pint water	2 tablespoons vinegar

1 Soak the rabbit for 1 hour in a bowl filled with cold water to which 2 tablespoons vinegar have been added. This sweetens and whitens the flesh.
2 Then with a sharp knife cut all meat from the bones, put this in water in a saucepan with salt and pepper and simmer gently for about 45 minutes.
3 Strain off the stock.
4 Line the basin with suet crust (see page 64). Roll the pieces of rabbit in the flour, mixed with good pinch salt, pepper and the sage.
5 Put alternate layers of rabbit and bacon into the suet pastry, cover with 1 gill rabbit stock and the rest of the suet pastry.
6 Continue as for steak and kidney pudding (see page 37) and cook in the same way.

Bacon stew

Use the same recipe as for haricot mutton (see page 32) but dice up piece of collar of bacon instead of the mutton. Flavour with a little sage and, if wished, serve with savoury dumplings.

Bacon and onion pudding

cooking time   2 hours

you will need:

8 oz. suet crust pastry
  (see page 64)

for the filling

8 oz. bacon	4–8 oz. onions
1 gill stock or water	good pinch salt, pepper

1 Chop bacon into pieces, peel and slice onions, sprinkle with salt and pepper.
2 Put into a basin lined with suet crust, add stock and cook in the same way as steak and kidney pudding (see page 37) but this will need only just over 2 hours cooking.

Bacon, mushroom and egg pie

cooking time   40 minutes

you will need:

8 oz. short crust pastry (see page 63)	2–4 oz. mushrooms (or mushrooms stalks)
4 good-sized rashers of bacon	2 eggs
small knob butter or margarine	1–2 teaspoons chopped parsley
	seasoning

1 Roll out pastry, use approximately half to line pie plate.
2 Using the extra butter or margarine, fry chopped bacon and mushrooms *lightly*.
3 Mix with the beaten eggs, parsley and seasoning.
4 Pour over pastry.
5 Cover with rest of pastry, seal the edges and decorate the top.
6 Brush with egg white—you will find a little left in the shell for this.
7 Bake in centre of hot oven (450°F.—Gas Mark 7) for 15–20 minutes, then lower heat to moderate for further 20 minutes.

Beef olives

cooking time   1½–2 hours

you will need:

1 lb. stewing beef— cut very thinly	2 oz. dripping
bay leaf	¾ pint brown sauce or brown gravy

for the stuffing

2 oz. fine breadcrumbs	¼ teaspoon mixed herbs
few drops lemon juice	
yolk of 1 egg	½ teaspoon chopped parsley
1 oz. suet or fat	

1 Cut the meat into neat squares.
2 Mix all ingredients for the stuffing together

then divide this between the pieces of meat and spread over.

3 Form into rolls or, if the squares of meat are sufficiently large, gather up into a dumpling shape or roll and secure with thin string or cotton.
4 Heat the dripping in a pan and fry the 'olives' in this until just brown on the outside.
5 Cover with a brown sauce, add the bay leaf.
6 Put a lid on the saucepan and simmer gently for 1½ hours or put into a covered casserole and simmer gently for 2 hours in a moderate oven.
7 To serve, arrange on a dish with a border of piped mashed potato and as many mixed vegetables as possible, cut into small dice before cooking.

Sweet corn beef casserole

cooking time   approximately 2¼ hours

you will need:

1 lb. stewing steak	1 pint stock (made with
salt	beef stock cube)
pepper	1 lb. carrots
2 level tablespoons flour	4 oz. mushrooms
1 oz. dripping	1 can sweet corn kernels
2 large sliced onions	

1 Trim meat and cut into 1-inch cubes.
2 Toss in the seasoning and flour.
3 Melt the dripping in a pan, and brown first the onions, then the meat. Remove them to a casserole.
4 Add the stock and peeled carrots. Cover the casserole and cook in the oven (325°F.—Gas Mark 3) for about 2 hours, or until meat is tender.
5 About 15 minutes before serving add the mushrooms and drained sweet corn.

Paprika beef pudding

cooking time   approximately 4½–5 hours

you will need:

for the pudding crust

10 oz. flour (with plain flour use 1½ level teaspoons baking powder)	4–5 oz. suet
	good pinch salt
	water to mix

for the filling

1–1¼ lb. stewing steak	little flour
2 or 3 tomatoes	1 or 2 teaspoons paprika
salt and pepper	pepper (the sweet red
water or stock	pepper)
2 large onions	

1 To make the pastry mix the flour and salt together, then add suet and enough water to make a soft pliable dough.
2 Roll out on floured board, and use most of the dough to line a greased basin, but save enough for the lid.
3 Cut the meat into neat pieces.
4 Put about a level tablespoon flour on to a plate, together with salt and pepper.
5 Roll the meat in this until well covered.
6 Slice the onions and tomatoes and mix together.
7 Fill the basin with the meat and vegetables, then add enough water or stock to come two-thirds up the basin.
8 Roll out the remaining pastry to the size of the top of the basin, moisten the edges of pastry and seal firmly.
9 Cover with greased greaseproof paper, putting a pleat across the centre of this to allow the pudding to rise.
10 Either use a second layer of greaseproof paper or cloth or aluminium foil.
11 Tie the paper and final covering on to the pudding or tuck round the edges firmly.
12 Put into a pan of boiling water and cook fairly rapidly for about 1½ hours, then lower the heat and cook gently for about 3 hours, or steam for approximately 5 hours.

Beef stew with dumplings

cooking time   approximately 2¼ hours

you will need:

1 lb. stewing steak	1 can condensed tomato
salt	soup or ¾ pint brown
pepper	stock
2 level tablespoons flour	1 gill water
	6 small onions
1 oz. dripping	3 potatoes

dumplings

3 oz. flour (with plain flour use 1 level teaspoon baking powder)	pinch of mixed herbs
	pepper
	1 oz. suet or margarine
	cold water
¼ teaspoon salt	

1 Cut meat into 1 inch cubes, removing excess fat.
2 Season with salt and pepper and toss in the flour.
3 Melt the dripping in a pan, add the meat and brown.
4 Pour in the can of condensed tomato soup and the water.
5 Stir well and allow to simmer for 1½ hours.
6 Add whole onions and the potatoes cut into 4 and simmer for a further 20 minutes.

To make the dumplings

7 Sieve flour, baking powder, salt, herbs and pepper into a basin.
8 Rub in the margarine or add suet and mix to a firm dough with water.
9 Divide into 8 and drop into the stew.
10 Simmer for a further 15 minutes with the lid on. Serve immediately.

Beef and onion pudding

cooking time $3\frac{1}{2}$–4 hours

you will need:

suet crust (see page 64)

for the filling

2 sliced and lightly fried onions	1–2 tablespoons chopped suet
1 lb. minced uncooked beef	3 oz. breadcrumbs seasoning
	1 egg

1 Line basin with the suet crust.
2 Mix all the filling ingredients together.
3 Pack into basin, cover with suet crust and steam for 2–$2\frac{1}{2}$ hours, very rapidly for the first hour and more slowly for a further $1\frac{1}{2}$ hours.

Butter bean and meat pudding

cooking time   3–4 hours

you will need:

8–10 oz. suet pastry
(see page 64)

filling

1 lb. stewing beef cut into small cubes	1 onion finely chopped or 1 heaped
1 small can butter beans or cooked butter beans	dessertspoon sliced onions
	salt and pepper

1 Use $\frac{3}{4}$ of the pastry to line a 2-pint greased basin.
2 Roll the remaining $\frac{1}{4}$ to form a lid.
3 Mix the meat, seasonings, onion and butter beans and use to fill the pastry-lined basin.
4 Damp the edges of the pastry lid and place on top of the pudding, sealing the edges.
5 Cover with greased greaseproof paper and steam for 3–4 hours.

Calf's head with brain sauce

cooking time   3 hours

1 Split the head down the centre.
2 Wash carefully and remove the brains.
3 Put the head, parsley, mixed herbs and bay leaves into a pan of cold water, just covering the head.
4 Bring just to the boil.
5 Remove any scum.
6 Put on the lid and simmer gently for about 3 hours.
7 When it is done take out all the meat.
8 Chop this neatly.
9 The tongue can be served separately or cut into neat fingers and added to the cooked meat when serving.

Brain sauce

$\frac{1}{2}$ pint white sauce (see page 90)	seasoning brain from calf's head

1 Soak the brain in cold water to which should be added a few drops of vinegar or lemon juice.

2 This will whiten it.
3 Simmer for 15 minutes in salted water.
4 Strain, chop and add to the white sauce.
5 To serve this dish: Arrange the meat from the head on to a hot dish. Pour over the brain sauce and garnish with snippets of crisp toast. Pig's or sheep's head can be used instead.

Calf's head brawn

cooking time $2\frac{1}{2}$–3 hours

you will need:

1 small calf's head	juice of $\frac{1}{2}$ lemon
seasoning	small bunch parsley
8 oz. stewing steak	pinch mixed herbs

1 Cook as in preceding recipe, but simmer for $1\frac{1}{2}$ hours.
2 Remove all the meat from the bones, cutting this meat into neat pieces.
3 Return this to the stock, together with diced steak and lemon juice.
4 Simmer gently for a further $1\frac{1}{2}$ hours.
5 Put the meat into a basin or mould.
6 Strain the liquid over it and leave to set.
7 Pig's or sheep's head can be used instead.
Note: A good sized calf's head can be split into two. Half could then be used in preceding recipe then the other half used in above recipe.

Cornish pasties

cooking time   50–60 minutes

you will need:

10 oz. short crust pastry (see page 63)	1 large onion
6 oz. uncooked rump steak or good quality stewing steak*	$\frac{1}{2}$ gill stock or gravy (or water flavoured with little yeast extract)
2 medium size potatoes or equivalent in small potatoes	salt and pepper mustard egg or milk to glaze

*Canned meat can be used instead in which case shorten the cooking time to approximately 35 minutes.

1 First make the pastry.
2 Roll this out to about $\frac{1}{4}$ inch thick, then cut into 4 rounds about the size of a large tea plate.
3 Cut the meat into tiny pieces then dice the potatoes and onion.
4 Mix these together, adding seasoning.
5 Put a good pile in the centre of each round and moisten with a little of the stock. Brush the edges of the pastry with water, then bring these together in the centre.
6 Press them tightly, so that there is no possibility of their opening during cooking and stand the pasties on a baking tray.
7 Brush the outside with either a little milk or beaten egg to give a slight glaze.

8 Bake in the centre of a hot oven (450°F.—Gas Mark 7) for about 25 minutes. Lower the heat to moderate (375–400°F. or Gas Mark 4) for a further 25–35 minutes to make sure the meat is cooked inside.

Egg and bacon pie

cooking time   approximately 35 minutes

you will need:

6 oz. short crust pastry   seasoning
  (see page 63)   3–4 eggs
4–6 oz. bacon

1 Line flan tin with pastry and bake for about 10 minutes in hot oven (425–450°F.—Gas Mark 6–7), to set, but not cook the pastry.
2 Fry diced bacon until just crisp.
3 Add to well beaten and seasoned eggs.
4 Pour the mixture into flan case.
5 Set for a further 25 minutes in a moderately hot oven.

Hamburger pie

cooking time

you will need:

8 oz. short crust pastry   2 oz. margarine or
  (see page 63)   butter
3 skinned tomatoes   2 finely chopped onions
½ gill milk   12 oz. minced beef
2 eggs   4 oz. grated cheese
seasoning

1 Line an 8 inch sandwich tin or flan ring with the pastry, building it up well at the sides.
2 Bake for 10 minutes 'blind' in a hot oven (450°F.—Gas Mark 7) but do not allow it to colour.
3 Meanwhile fry the onions in the butter, add the tomatoes, minced beef, and mix thoroughly.
4 Stir in the milk and seasoning and blend well.
5 Spread over the pastry.
6 Beat and season the eggs, add the cheese and pour carefully over the beef filling.
7 Bake for approximately 45 minutes in the centre of a moderate oven (375°F.—Gas Mark 4). *Note:* Choose a good quality beef for this recipe. If using less good quality it is advisable to cook for a short while with the onions and tomatoes before putting into the pastry. Cooked minced beef can be used, but does not give such a moist filling.

Hamburgers

cooking time   frying 10 minutes
        baking 30 minutes
you will need:

1 lb. minced beef   1 heaped teaspoon
1 good-sized potato   chopped parsley
1 large or 2 medium-   1 teaspoon Worcestershire
  sized onions   sauce
½ teaspoon mixed   seasoning
  herbs

1 Put meat into a basin, add grated onion, seasoning, herbs, parsley and sauce.
2 Lastly grate in raw peeled potato.
3 Mix thoroughly together.
4 There will be no need to add liquid as the potato binds the mixture together.
5 Form into large flat cakes and either fry steadily in hot fat or bake on a well greased tin for about 25–30 minutes in a moderately hot oven (400°F.—Gas Mark 5).
6 The cakes can be floured or tossed in crisp breadcrumbs before cooking—don't try to turn into a neat rissole shape.
7 Serve hot and, if wished, with a fried egg on top.

Boiled mutton and caper sauce

cooking time   1½–2 hours

you will need:

1–1¼ lb. scrag or   caper sauce (see
  middle neck of mutton   page 89)
seasoning   onions

1 Put the meat into the pan with the vegetables.
2 Cover with cold water, bring to the boil, skim.
3 Add seasoning, lower the heat and simmer gently for approximately 1½–2 hours.
4 Lift meat and vegetables on to a hot dish and make the caper sauce using half milk and half the mutton stock. Extra mutton stock can be served separately.

Haricot mutton

cooking time   2¼ hours

you will need:

1 lb. mutton (use best   4 small carrots
  end of neck, leg or   1 large onion
  shoulder)   6 oz. haricot beans
1 oz. lard   salt
1 pint water or stock   a few potatoes
pepper   1 oz. flour

1 Soak haricot beans overnight in cold water.
2 Heat the lard in saucepan and fry sliced onion and pieces of meat for a few minutes.
3 Stir in the flour and cook gently for about 5 minutes, stirring all the time.
4 Gradually add the cold water, bring to the boil, stir well until it has boiled and thickened slightly.
5 Add the carrots, salt and pepper and haricot beans, well drained.
6 Simmer gently for nearly 2 hours.
7 Slice the potatoes and put them, with seasoning, on top of the mutton stew adding a good pinch of salt and pepper.
8 Cook for a further 25 minutes until potatoes are tender.
9 To dish up lift sliced potatoes carefully from the stew, put on a hot dish and pour haricot mutton on top.

Stewed kidneys

cooking time   20 minutes

you will need:

2 onions	½ tablespoon
1 oz. flour	concentrated tomato
4 lambs' kidneys	purée (or use 2
2 or 3 rashers bacon	tomatoes)
seasoning	½ pint brown stock (or
parsley	water with a little beef
1½ oz. margarine or fat	or yeast extract)
cooked rice	

1 Slice the onions very thinly.
2 Fry in the hot margarine together with the diced bacon (care should be taken NOT to brown the onions).
3 Remove fat from kidneys and cut into neat pieces.
4 Add the diced kidneys to the onions and cook for several minutes.
5 Blend in the flour and when this has been thoroughly absorbed, gradually add the stock.
6 Bring to the boil, stirring well, and cook until smooth.
7 Season, add tomato purée and simmer for 10 minutes.
8 Serve in a border of cooked rice. Garnish with parsley.

Spiced lamb stew

cooking time   nearly 2 hours

you will need:

1½–2 lb. breast of	1 green pepper (if
lamb or scrag end of	available)
neck cut into pieces	¼ crushed clove garlic
4 oz. diced celery	(this can be omitted)
3 large tomatoes	good pinch paprika
salt	pepper
pepper	good pinch mixed spice
water	2 oz. rice
chopped parsley	1 oz. fat
1 large onion	paprika pepper to garnish

1 Fry the onion in the hot fat for a few minutes.
2 Add garlic, if using this.
3 Fry pieces of lamb also for a few minutes, then cover with cold water.
4 Add seasonings and vegetables.
5 Simmer gently for about 1½ hours. Add rice.
6 Continue cooking for a further 20 minutes, making sure the liquid does not evaporate too much. Taste and re-season if necessary.
7 Garnish with the parsley and paprika pepper.

Lamb chops in spicy tomato sauce

cooking time   approximately 45 minutes

you will need:

4 lamb chops	½ oz. butter or margarine

½ pint spicy tomato sauce

1 medium-sized onion	1 can condensed
(finely chopped)	tomato soup

1 oz. butter	¼ teaspoon made
1 dessertspoon sugar	mustard
1 dessertspoon lemon	salt
juice	pepper
1 dessertspoon Wor-	
cestershire sauce	

1 Trim excess fat from chops, bone and roll.
2 Melt the butter in a pan and fry the chops until brown on both sides.
3 Pour on the spicy tomato sauce.
4 Cover and simmer gently for 35–40 minutes until tender.

To make spicy tomato sauce

1 Cook onion gently in melted butter until tender.
2 Pour the condensed tomato soup and other ingredients into the onion and, stirring, heat gently for 1 minute.

Stuffed breast of lamb

cooking time   2 hours

you will need:

1 boned breast of lamb	lemon juice or garlic
(about 2 lb.)	2 tablespoons flour
salt and pepper	

stuffing

½ oz. dripping or butter	1 teaspoon chopped
1 cooking apple	parsley
8 oz. sausage meat	rosemary
2 tablespoons fresh	1 teaspoon finely
breadcrumbs	chopped mint or
lemon juice or garlic	½ teaspoon mixed
2 tablespoons flour	herbs

1 Prepare the stuffing by melting dripping or butter.
2 Lightly fry the apple (peeled, cored and chopped) and the sausage meat.
3 Cook for 2–3 minutes, then stir in the other ingredients.
4 Wipe the lamb.
5 Sprinkle the inside with a little salt, pepper and lemon juice or rub over with garlic.
6 Spread with the stuffing.
7 Roll it up and tie with string or secure with metal skewers.
8 Mix a pinch of salt and pepper with flour and rub this into the surface of the lamb.
9 Place in a shallow baking dish and cook (300°F.—Gas Mark 2) for about 2 hours.
10 Serve with creamed potatoes, peas and apple sauce.

Lamb casserole

cooking time   2 hours

you will need:

1 breast of lamb	stuffing (see above)
approx. 1½ lb. mixed	or for a change use
root vegetables	2–3 oz. cooked rice
seasoning	instead of breadcrumbs
	little water

1 Stuff the lamb, roll firmly and secure with cotton or skewer.
2 Slice the root vegetables fairly thinly and put at the bottom of a casserole, seasoning well and adding a very little water.
3 Put the meat on top and cook as before.
4 When serving put the meat on to a hot dish, arranging the strained vegetables round it, and use any liquid left for a thickened gravy.

Breast of lamb Italienne

cooking time   2 hours

you will need:

1 breast of lamb	2 tablespoons parsley
pinch mixed herbs	(chopped finely)
1 oz. margarine	little chopped celery
egg or milk to bind	3–4 oz. cooked macaroni
2 thinly sliced onions	2 tomatoes
4 oz. soft breadcrumbs	

1 Mix the cooked macaroni with the sliced onion and tomatoes.
2 Season and arrange at the bottom of a greased baking dish or casserole.
3 Make the stuffing for the meat by mixing the breadcrumbs, parsley, mixed herbs, chopped celery and margarine together.
4 Add the egg or just enough milk to bind.
5 Spread the meat with the stuffing and roll firmly.
6 Tie or skewer into position.
7 Put the meat on top of the macaroni mixture.
8 Cover the dish and bake for about $1\frac{1}{4}$–$1\frac{1}{2}$ hours in the centre of a moderately hot oven (400°F.—Gas Mark 5).
9 After about 30–45 minutes stir any fat that has dropped into the macaroni mixture to keep it moist, reduce heat at same time.

Braised lamb with baby turnips

cooking time   approximately $1\frac{3}{4}$ hours

you will need:

2 lb. lean lamb taken	$\frac{1}{2}$ tablespoon chopped
from leg or shoulder	parsley
$\frac{3}{4}$ tablespoon turmeric*	1 sweet green pepper
$\frac{1}{2}$ teaspoon dried basil	6 oz. butter
1 tablespoon chopped	1 jar yoghourt (about
mint leaves	4–5 oz.)
8 small onions	1 lb. young turnips

*If wished you can use curry powder. Add $1\frac{1}{2}$ tablespoons of this powder with chopped mint leaves, parsley and green pepper.

1 Wash and dry the turnips.
2 Slice them in half lengthways, but do not completely sever the two halves.
3 Chop the green pepper and peel the onions.
4 Put the yoghourt into a heavy saucepan with the turmeric and basil.
5 Cut the lamb into cubes about 2 inches in size.
6 Add to the pan and stir well.
7 Bring to the boil over a fierce heat.

8 As soon as the mixture becomes dry, add the butter.
9 Now fry the lamb over a gentle heat for 6–8 minutes.
10 Add the chopped mint leaves, whole onions, turnips, green pepper and salt.
11 Add 1 pint of stock or water, stir well and cover.
12 Simmer gently for about $1\frac{1}{2}$ hours until the turnips are tender.
13 Sprinkle with the chopped parsley and serve.

Lancashire hot pot

cooking time $1\frac{1}{2}$–2 hours

you will need:

12 oz.–1 lb. lean	hot water
middle or best end	salt
mutton or stewing steak	pepper
2 large onions	1 oz. margarine
1 lb. potatoes	parsley

1 Cut the meat into neat pieces.
2 Peel and slice the potatoes and onions. They should be about $\frac{1}{4}$ inch thick.
3 Fill a casserole with alternate layers of meat, onions, potato.
4 You should end with a layer of potato.
5 Sprinkle salt and pepper over each layer.
6 Pour enough hot water into the casserole to about half fill.
7 Put the margarine on top in small pieces and put on the lid.
8 If the casserole hasn't a lid, then spread the margarine over greaseproof paper and tuck this securely over the top.
9 Bake in the coolest part of the oven, either for 2 hours at 350°F.—Gas Mark 3, or for a good $1\frac{1}{4}$ hours at 375°F.—Gas Mark 4.
10 Take lid or paper off for the last 20 minutes to brown the top.
11 Garnish with a little parsley.

Liver and onion ring

cooking time   approximately 45 minutes

you will need:

8 oz. American biscuit	$\frac{1}{2}$ level teaspoon
crust pastry (see page 62)	marjoram
	good pinch pepper
egg or milk to glaze	3 tablespoons tomato
8 oz. liver	ketchup
1 level teaspoon salt	$\frac{1}{2}$ teaspoon Worcester-
$\frac{3}{4}$ level teaspoon celery	shire sauce
salt	$\frac{1}{2}$ pint tomato sauce
2 oz. onions	(see page 89)

1 Place the liver in a small saucepan and just cover with water.
2 Season and simmer for approximately 15 minutes.
3 Drain.
4 Mince or chop finely, adding salt, celery salt,

marjoram, pepper, tomato ketchup and Worcestershire sauce.

5 Chop the onions finely and boil for a few minutes in salted water.
6 Strain and add to the other ingredients.
7 Make the pastry.
8 Roll out to a rectangle 9 x 11 inches.
9 Spread with the liver mixture.
0 Roll up, starting from the 11 inch side.
1 Seal the edges.
2 Place on a baking sheet well brushed with vegetable shortening and shape into a ring.
3 Join the ends together. Take a pair of scissors and cut through the pastry at 2 inch intervals to within 1 inch of the ring centre.
4 The ring can then be served whole or cut in slices. Brush with milk or egg.
5 Bake in centre of hot oven (450°F.—Gas Mark 7) for 20–30 minutes.
6 Serve hot with sauce.

Meat mould

cooking time   1½ hours

you will need:

12 oz. streaky bacon	8 oz. minced beef
3 oz. breadcrumbs	grated nutmeg
pepper	salt
1 gill stock	1 egg

1 Mince the bacon and add the minced beef, breadcrumbs and seasoning.
2 Pour in the stock and beaten egg.
3 Beat the mixture well and turn into a greased basin.
4 Cover the basin with greaseproof paper and boil or steam for 1½ hours.
5 Turn out when cold and serve on a bed of lettuce and tomatoes.

Mince collops

cooking time   approximately 1 hour

you will need:

1–1¼ lb. minced beef	1 oz. flour
2 tomatoes (or a tablespoon tomato purée)	½ pint stock (or water flavoured with a little yeast extract or bouillon cube)
2 onions	
squeeze lemon juice	**to garnish**
2 oz. fat	mixed root vegetables

1 Chop the onions finely and fry in the hot fat, then work in the flour and cook gently for a few minutes.
2 Take the pan off the heat, and add the stock gradually, bringing to the boil and cooking until a smooth thick sauce.
3 Break up the lumps of minced beef with your fork, then put into the sauce. Continue to cook gently, stirring from time to time with a wooden spoon, for the meat still tends to form large lumps at the beginning of cooking.

4 When quite smooth add the skinned and chopped tomatoes or tomato purée and seasoning.
5 Put the lid on the pan and simmer for 45 minutes.
6 If necessary, add a little more stock, but this dish is better when rather stiff. Put on to a hot dish and garnish with diced cooked vegetables.
7 Just before serving add the lemon juice.

Devilled mince
Fry the onion in the fat, then work in 1 or 2 teaspoons curry powder. Add meat etc., together with 1 tablespoon chutney, few sultanas, pinch sugar as well as seasoning.

Spanish mince
Fry the onions and a crushed clove of garlic in the fat. When adding the tomatoes, also add chopped green or red pepper, or chopped celery and diced carrots and peas. Stir in 1 or 2 oz. cooked rice before serving.

Mutton pies

cooking time   approximately 40 minutes

you will need:

8 oz. short crust pastry (see page 63)

filling

1 lb. scrag end of mutton	1 small finely chopped onion
1 medium potato	1 oz. seasoned flour
egg to glaze	

1 Make the pastry and roll out thinly.
2 Cut into rounds and line 12 small deep patty tins, reserving some pastry for the lids.

To make the filling:
3 Bone mutton, remove excess fat, cut meat and potatoes into small dice, mix with onion and toss in seasoned flour.
4 Fill each pastry case with meat mixture.
5 Damp edges and cover with pastry lids.
6 Press edges together, flute and make a small cross-slit in top of each to allow steam to escape.
7 Brush with beaten egg.
8 Bake in a hot oven (425°F.—Gas Mark 6) for 35–40 minutes.
9 Serve hot or cold.

Oxtail

cooking time   2–3 hours

you will need:

1 good sized or 2 medium ox tails	2 onions
	2 carrots
1 oz. flour	2 oz. dripping
1 pint water or stock	seasoning

1 If the butcher has not jointed the tails you must cut them into neat pieces.

2 Heat the dripping in a pan and fry sliced onions and carrots in this.
3 Lift out.
4 Coat the pieces of oxtail in well seasoned flour.
5 Fry these in the remaining dripping until lightly brown.
6 Return the vegetables to the pan together with the stock.
7 Bring to the boil.
8 Add seasoning and simmer gently for 2–3 hours.
9 For many people this is rather 'fatty' and so it is a good idea to prepare it the day before, take off the surplus fat and re-heat.
10 Soaked haricot or butter beans can also be added, in which case you will need a little extra liquid.

Ox tongue

cooking time   2–3 hours

1 Ask for a salted tongue and soak several hours, or overnight, in cold water. (If it is not possible to obtain a salted tongue then cook at once, adding salt to taste. The colour is never as good, though, as when salted or pickled.)
2 When ready to cook put into cold water, bring to the boil, add onion, carrot, bay leaf.
3 Simmer very gently in covered pan allowing 40 minutes per lb.
4 At the end of this time lift tongue out of stock and allow to cool until you can handle it.
5 Meanwhile, boil stock in open pan until only about 1–1½ gills.
6 Remove skin of tongue and any tiny bones at the root of the tongue.
7 Lift into a round cake tin or saucepan, curling it round to give a good shape. It needs to be a fairly tight fit.
8 Dissolve 1 level teaspoon powder gelatine in the stock, strain over the tongue.
9 Put a plate or weight over top to press into shape, and leave until cold.
10 Remove weight etc., dip base of tin or saucepan into hot water for ½ minute to loosen the jelly round the meat and turn out.

Pigs in blankets

cooking time   20 minutes

you will need:

6 large sausages	6 oz. short or flaky pastry
6 small fingers of cheese (can be left out)	(see page 63)

1 Split the sausages and insert the fingers of cheese.
2 Roll out the pastry and cut into 6 squares.

3 Lay 1 sausage on each square, diagonally, then pick up the corners and bring together, so that the ends of the sausages are 'exposed'.
4 Brush with little milk or egg and bake for about 20 minutes in the centre of a hot oven (450–475°F.—Gas Mark 7–8). Use the greater heat for flaky pastry.
5 Serve hot with tomatoes.

Pork pies

cooking time   approximately 45 minutes

you will need:

12 oz. hot water crust pastry (see below)

filling

1 lb. lean pork	stock
½ level teaspoon salt	egg or milk for glazing
¼ level teaspoon pepper	1 rounded teaspoon
pinch mixed herbs	gelatine
2 hard-boiled eggs	1 gill water or stock

1 Make the pastry.
2 Divide the mixture into 6 and from each take ⅓ for the lids.
3 Mould the pastry into a small pie shape with the hands or if preferred round a small tin or tumbler.
4 Place round each a double band of greaseproof paper and tie firmly with a piece of string.
5 Cut lids to fit.
6 Cut the pork into small cubes and sprinkle it with salt, pepper and herbs.
7 Add slices of hard-boiled egg.
8 Place the pork mixture inside each pie case, brush round the edge with water.
9 Add a little stock made by boiling bones, or water.
10 Put on lid and flute round the edge.
11 Make a hole in the centre.
12 Decorate with pastry tassels or leaves, as desired.
13 Bake in the centre of a moderately hot oven (400°F.—Gas Mark 5) for 40–45 minutes.
14 After cooking for 30 minutes, remove the paper and brush the sides with egg or milk.
15 Continue cooking.
16 If possible, when the pies are cooked and cooled add jellied pork stock as below:
17 Dissolve the gelatine in the stock.
18 Add little meat extract, if liked.
19 Allow to cool.
20 Just before setting pour into each cooled pie through the centre hole.
21 Leave to set before cutting.

Hot water crust pastry for raised pies

you will need:

12 oz. plain flour	¼ pint water
3–4 oz. fat	pinch salt

1 Sieve flour and salt together.
2 Melt fat in warm water and add to flour.
3 Mix with knife and knead gently with fingers.
4 Use when warm.

American rice lamb skillet

cooking time   approximately 45 minutes

you will need:

6 lamb chops	1 large onion
1 teaspoon fat	1 tablespoon parsley
1 pint beef stock or	1–2 tablespoons brown
water and meat extract	sugar
4 oz. uncooked rice	1 teaspoon salt
8 oz. dried apricots	$\frac{1}{8}$ teaspoon pepper

1 Chop or mince onion, parsley and apricots.
2 Trim off excess fat from chops.
3 In a heavy iron pan brown chops in heated fat.
4 Remove chops and drain off all excess fat. Pan will be almost dry.
5 Add onions and parsley.
6 Sauté until tender but not brown.
7 Pour in beef stock and bring to boil.
8 Add remaining ingredients and return to a boil.
9 Place chops on top, cover with a tight fitting lid or aluminium foil.
0 Simmer over low heat for 30 minutes or until chops are tender.

Sausage and vegetable savoury

cooking time   30 minutes

you will need:

1 oz. margarine	1 can vegetable soup
4 rashers bacon	salt
1 lb. pork sausages	pepper
1½ lb. potatoes	

1 Cook the potatoes and mash them with the margarine.
2 Cut bacon into small pieces and fry gently until crisp.
3 Remove.
4 Fry sausages for approximately 15–20 minutes.
5 Put a layer of potatoes into a deep dish.
6 Cover with sausages and bacon.
7 Pour over gently heated, seasoned vegetable soup.

Sausage and oatmeal pudding

cooking time $2\frac{1}{2}$ hours

you will need:

8 oz. suet crust (see page 64)

for the filling

1 lb. sausage meat	little stock
good pinch powdered	2 grated onions
sage	3 oz. fine oatmeal
seasoning	1 egg

1 Line the basin with suet crust.
2 Mix all ingredients for the filling together and bind with beaten egg and stock.

3 Put this into the basin and cover with a lid of crust.
4 Steam rapidly for 1 hour, then more slowly for a further 1½ hours.
5 Serve with good brown gravy and vegetables.

Lamb toad-in-the-hole

cooking time   40 minutes

you will need:

4 small lamb chops	pancake batter (see page
2 tomatoes	60)
	small knob of fat

1 Make the batter.
2 Heat the knob of fat in a Yorkshire pudding or baking dish.
3 Add the chops and halved tomatoes.
4 Cook for 10 minutes in a hot oven (450° F.—Gas Mark 7).
5 Pour over the batter. Return to the oven.
6 After 20 minutes the heat can be lowered slightly for the remaining 10 minutes. Serve at once.

Sausage toad-in-the-hole

cooking time   40–45 minutes

As lamb toad-in-the-hole but use 12 oz.–1 lb. sausages, cooking these for 10 minutes if large, or 5 minutes if small.

Steak and kidney pudding

cooking time   4 hours

you will need:

8 oz. suet crust pastry (see page 64)

for the filling

12 oz.–1 lb. stewing	2 lamb's kidneys or
steak	3–4 oz. ox kidney
seasoning	little extra flour
water or stock	

1 Roll out pastry on floured board with a lightly floured rolling pin until it is less than $\frac{1}{4}$ inch thick.
2 Put pieces of pastry into a $1\frac{1}{4}$–$1\frac{1}{2}$ pint basin and press it against the sides. Try to keep pastry flat without folds otherwise the pudding crust will be too thick.
3 Cut off surplus as this will make the lid.
4 Cut steak into thin pieces and dice the kidney.
5 Mix together 1 level tablespoon flour and a good pinch of salt.
6 Put a layer of meat into the pudding, then a sprinkling of the seasoned flour. Fill the basin in this way until all meat is used.
7 Cover with enough water or stock to nearly fill basin.
8 Re-roll the last of the pastry and make into a round large enough to cover top of basin.
9 Put this over the pudding, press edges of lid to edges of side of the pastry.

10 Cover with a piece of greased paper, greasy side against pudding.
11 Put into a steamer over a pan of boiling water and cook for about 3½–4 hours or even longer.. For the first 2 hours the water must boil rapidly under the pudding.
12 Fill up with boiling water as it gets low.
13 If you have no steamer, stand the pudding in a saucepan with the water coming half way up the basin.
14 Fill up frequently.
15 When pudding is cooked, lift from steamer on to kitchen table, then lift on to a hot plate.
16 Tie a napkin round the basin.
17 Heat a little more stock, or the water from cooking a cabbage and put into a sauce boat.
18 When the first slice of the pudding is cut out, pour in the stock to give more gravy.

Steak and kidney pie

cooking time   nearly 2 hours or about 1 hour if meat is pre-cooked

you will need:

12 oz.–1 lb. stewing steak	2 lamb's or sheep's kidneys or about 4 oz. ox kidney
1 level tablespoon flour	½ teaspoon salt
good pinch pepper	water or stock
6 oz. short crust or flaky pastry (see page 63)	

1 Cut the steak and kidney into small pieces and roll in the seasoned flour.
2 Put the meat into a pie dish or individual dishes, seeing that the kidney is well distributed.
3 Pour over enough water or stock to come half-way up the meat, any more would boil out in cooking.

With flaky pastry

1 Roll out the pastry and cover the pie.
2 Decorate and glaze.
3 Bake in the centre of a hot oven (450°F.—Gas Mark 7) for about 25 minutes to give the pastry a chance to rise.
4 Put a piece of paper over the top and lower the heat to very moderate (350°F.—Gas Mark 3) to make sure the meat is cooked.
5 Give it about a further 1½ hours.
6 When serving have a sauce boat of hot stock available to pour into the pie to make extra gravy if you wish.

With short crust pastry

If using this type of crust, it is probably better to pre-cook the meat as in chicken pie (see page 43), then bake for 1 hour only.

Chinese or Malayan sweet and sour pork

cooking time   approximately 15–20 minutes

you will need:

8–12 oz. loin of pork

sweet and sour sauce

1 level tablespoon cornflour	5 tablespoons water or stock
2 tablespoons malt vinegar	1 level tablespoon sweet pickle
1 level dessertspoon sugar	½ tablespoon lemon juice
1 level dessertspoon golden syrup	1 tablespoon tomato ketchup
	1 tablespoon sherry (optional)
	1 oz. fat

batter

1 egg	fat or oil for frying
1 level tablespoon plain flour	1 level tablespoon cornflour

1 Blend the cornflour and vinegar together.
2 Place all the sauce ingredients in a saucepan.
3 Stir well.
4 Bring to the boil and simmer gently for 5 minutes.
5 Cut the pork into ¾–1 inch squares.
6 Fry in the fat for 5–10 minutes until brown.

To make the batter

7 Lightly whisk the egg, flour and cornflour together.
8 Dip the cooked pork in the batter.
9 Fry for 2–3 minutes in a pan of fat heated to 360°F. (or until a 1-inch cube of day-old bread turns golden brown in 1 minute).
10 Drain on tissue paper.
11 Serve with the sweet and sour sauce on a bed of fried or boiled rice.

Swedish meat balls

cooking time   approximately 20 minutes

you will need:

3 oz. butter (or blend of butter and olive oil)	1½ lb. meat mixture (ideally one should use 8 oz. beef, 8 oz. pork, 8 oz. veal minced together)
1 onion (chopped)	
2–3 oz. breadcrumbs	
2 tablespoons top milk, (or unsweetened evaporated milk)	1 large egg (or small egg and extra yolk)
1 teaspoon salt	1 dessertspoon chopped parsley
¼ teaspoon pepper— preferably black	1 heaped teaspoon flour
1 tablespoon tomato ketchup	1 gill thin cream (coffee cream) or evaporated milk

1 Melt half the butter (or blend of butter and oil).
2 When hot lightly fry onion until soft but not browned.
3 Soak crumbs (using top milk or evaporated milk).
4 Mix with meat in a bowl.

5 Add cooked onions, seasonings, beaten egg and parsley, mixing well together.

6 Divide mixture with floured hands, forming shapes the size of golf balls.

7 Heat remaining fat and fry the balls a rich brown colour, shaking pan frequently to turn them, and adding extra fat as required.

8 Drain when cooked, arrange on hot dish and keep hot.

9 Add flour to fat remaining in pan and mix well.

10 Stir in gradually the thin cream or evaporated milk, mixing well, and then the tomato ketchup, increasing the quantity to taste, as required.

11 When sauce is smooth and creamy strain over meat balls.

Creamed sweetbreads

cooking time   30 minutes

you will need:

12 oz.–1 lb. sweetbreads	$\frac{3}{4}$ gill white stock or white stock and milk
little lemon juice	1 oz. flour
seasoning	1 tablespoon milk
2 tablespoons cream	

1 First soak the sweetbreads in cold water for 1 hour.

2 Put into a saucepan and cover with more cold water.

3 Bring the water to the boil and throw it away.

4 This process is known as 'blanching' the sweetbread and whitens it.

5 Return the sweetbread to the saucepan with the liquid, lemon juice and seasoning.

6 Simmer gently for about 15–20 minutes.

7 Remove sweetbread and take off any skin.

8 Blend the flour with 1 tablespoon cold milk, add to stock, then bring to the boil and cook until thickened.

9 Lastly stir in the cream.

Fried sweetbreads

cooking time   approximately 30 minutes

you will need:

1 lb. lamb's sweetbreads	water to cover
butter or margarine for frying	seasoning

to coat

1 egg mixed with little water	breadcrumbs
	flour

1 Wash the sweetbreads well, then soak in cold water for 1 hour.

2 Put into saucepan, cover with water.

3 Bring to the boil and simmer for 2 or 3 minutes.

4 Strain off the water. This is essential to blanch the sweetbreads and make them a good colour.

5 Place in a saucepan again and add water and seasoning.

6 Simmer for 15 minutes.

7 Strain and press between 2 plates.

8 Cut into neat slices when cold and firm.

9 Dip first in a little flour, then in egg and breadcrumbs, and fry in hot butter or margarine.

10 Serve with jacket potatoes and Brussels sprouts.

Tripe and onions

cooking time $1\frac{1}{4}$–$1\frac{1}{2}$ hours

you will need:

1$\frac{1}{2}$ lb. tripe	2 large onions
1 oz. butter or margarine	$\frac{1}{2}$ pint milk
	1 oz. flour
parsley	seasoning
red (paprika) pepper	

1 Cut the tripe into neat pieces.

2 Put into a pan of cold water, bring to the boil, throw away the water. This improves the colour of the tripe.

3 Put the tripe with 1 gill milk and $\frac{1}{2}$ pint water, the thinly sliced onions and seasoning into a pan and simmer gently until tender.

4 This takes about 1 hour.

5 Blend the flour with the remainder of the milk, add to the tripe, bring to the boil and cook until smooth.

6 Add the butter and a little extra seasoning if required.

7 Garnish with chopped parsley and paprika pepper.

Breast of veal with prune and anchovy stuffing

cooking time $1\frac{1}{4}$ hours

you will need:

1 small or $\frac{1}{2}$ larger breast of veal (boned)	8 oz. dried prunes (previously soaked in water)
1 small can anchovies	

1 First bring the prunes to the boil, then stone them.

2 Cut about 4 of the anchovy fillets in half lengthways, then soak them in milk for about 20 minutes to remove excess salt.

3 Chop up remaining anchovies and mix with the chopped prunes.

4 Spread French mustard over veal then pile on the stuffing.

5 Roll firmly and secure with string or skewers.

6 Arrange the remaining anchovies in a lattice pattern over the top.

7 Roast in a moderate oven (375°F.—Gas Mark 4) for about $1\frac{1}{4}$ hours—according to the size of the joint.

8 Serve with roast potatoes and Brussels sprouts.

Barbecued veal

cooking time   approximately 2 hours

you will need:

1¼–1½ lb. stewing veal cut into neat pieces, or use veal chops instead	water
	3 large onions
	2 eating apples
	2 teaspoons sugar
seasoning—including a good pinch dry mustard	1 or 2 oz. margarine
	2 tablespoons vinegar or lemon juice
1 oz. flour	2 bay leaves
½ gill cooking Burgundy (not essential)	good pinch mixed herbs seasoning for sauce

1 Cut the veal into small pieces, wash and dry well.
2 Put into a saucepan, just covering with cold water, add seasoning, bay leaves and mixed herbs, bring to the boil and skim thoroughly.
3 Lower heat and cook gently for 1½ hours.
4 Remove veal from liquid and measure off a good pint of stock.
5 Heat margarine in saucepan and when very hot fry onions, cut into neat rings, until just softened but neither broken nor browned.
6 Mix in the flour.
7 Take saucepan off the heat and gradually add 1 pint of the veal stock, stirring the whole time.
8 Bring the sauce to the boil and stir until slightly thickened.
9 Add seasoning, sugar, lemon juice or vinegar.
10 Put pieces of veal into the sauce and cook very slowly for 15–20 minutes.
11 Cut the apples into rings, taking out the cores and pips but leaving them with the skins still on, particularly if these are a bright colour.
12 Simmer for 5 minutes only.
13 Lastly stir in the Burgundy, although the dish still has a good flavour if this is left out.
14 Arrange the veal on a dish with the sauce and the rings of apple and onion on top.

Devilled casserole of veal with vegetables and bacon rolls

cooking time   1½–1¾ hours

you will need:

1½ lb. stewing veal	2 tablespoons tomato ketchup
2 oz. butter or margarine	1 liberal teaspoon made mustard
1 oz. flour	½ level teaspoon salt
½ pint water	8 small or 4 large sized carrots
sprinkling of pepper	
6 small tomatoes	
2 bacon rashers	

1 Cut the veal into cubes and brown in the heated fat.
2 Lift into a casserole. Stir the flour into the fat and cook, stirring, until brown.

3 Stir in the water, ketchup, mustard, salt and pepper and bring to the boil.
4 Pour over the meat in the casserole, add carrots and cover.
5 Cook in a very moderate oven (350°F.—Gas Mark 3) for about 1 hour.
6 Pour boiling water over tomatoes, drain and peel off skin.
7 Place tomatoes in the casserole and add also the bacon, first halving and trimming and rolling the rashers.
8 Cook a further 30 minutes, removing the lid after 15 minutes.
Note: Cubed stewing steak can also be cooked this way, without the bacon.

Veal olives

As beef olives (see page 29) but use stewing veal instead. Add plenty of lemon thyme to the stuffing and a little chopped thyme to the gravy too.

To cook Yorkshire pudding

cooking time   15–40 minutes

you will need:

pancake batter (see page 60)

It may be necessary to raise heat of oven before putting Yorkshire pudding in to cook and for first 5–10 minutes cooking time, if you are afraid beef may get overcooked take it out for a few minutes.

1 Make batter and leave standing until ready to cook.
2 When ready to cook put a knob of lard or dripping into a Yorkshire pudding tin (measuring about 7 x 5 inches) and heat in oven for a few minutes.
3 Pour in the batter and cook for about 30 minutes in a hot oven.
4 In every type of cooker use the top of the oven which is the hottest position.
5 To save cooking time you can cook the batter in small patty tins. Put a piece of fat (the size of a large pea) in each tin, heat this.
6 Pour in the batter and cook for about 15–20 minutes at the top of a hot oven.
7 Another way of cooking Yorkshire pudding is in the meat tin.
8 Pour away most of the fat, pour in batter, then stand meat on trivet and put on rack above pudding. This will take about 40 minutes cooking time.

Chapter 6
Main Meal—Poultry

Due to intensive breeding, poultry has now become a reasonable price and it is worth buying on many occasions. Poultry when young and tender should not be over-cooked, as over-cooked poultry is not only spoiled in flavour, but extremely difficult to carve. Poultry for casserole dishes should be cooked very slowly, unless in a pressure cooker, so that it becomes tender without being hardened in any way.

Poultry Cooking Guide

type	how to cook	accompaniments
chicken	Young fowls should be roasted in moderate oven. Allow 15 minutes for each lb. and 15 minutes over. For roasting see page 42. For other methods see page 43. Small broilers can be used for frying and grilling (see page 43).	Veal stuffing, bread sauce, sausages and bacon rolls, green salad.
duck	Roasted—15 minutes per lb. and 15 minutes over. Start in a hot oven, then reduce to moderate (see page 42).	Sage and onion stuffing. Apple sauce, thick brown gravy or orange and port wine sauce, orange salad.
goose	As duck (see page 42).	As duck.
guinea fowl	As chicken (see page 42).	As chicken.
turkey	Roast in moderate oven 15 minutes per lb. and 15 minutes over for a bird under 12 lb. 12 minutes per lb. and 12 minutes over for a bird over 12 lb. (see page 42).	Veal stuffing, bread sauce, sausages, brown sauce, salads.

Frozen poultry

There is a great deal of frozen poultry on the market today and since it is prime quality it is well worth buying. The best results are obtained if the poultry is allowed to thaw out gradually. Do not attempt to de-frost it by immersing in hot water and do not cook when it is frozen.

Very slow roasting poultry including turkey

1 Allow 1¼ hours for first pound and then 25 minutes over up to 7 lb. and 20 minutes a lb. after that.
2 A 5 lb. bird takes 2 hours 55 minutes, but a 10 lb. bird takes 4 hours 45 minutes.
3 Roast in a very slow oven (250–275°F.–Gas Mark ¼–1).

4 To brown bird raise temperature of oven for the last 25 minutes.
5 This is an excellent way of cooking if in doubt as to tenderness of bird.

How to draw poultry or game

1 First cut off the feet, and if necessary draw the sinews from the legs.
2 Hold the bird by the legs and singe if desired.
3 Cut off the head, leaving about 3 inches of neck.
4 Insert a small pointed knife at the end of the spine and split up the skin of the neck. Pull away loose skin, then cut off the neck close to the shoulder. Keep the neck.
5 Remove the crop and windpipe.
6 Cut round the vent. Put in fingers and loosen the inside. Do this carefully so that the gall bladder (attached to the liver) is not broken.

7 Firmly draw out all the inside.
8 Cut gall bladder from the liver.
9 Put the neck, liver, gizzard, heart and kidneys into bowl of cold water. Wash thoroughly, then simmer these gently to make stock for gravy.
10 Wipe inside of bird with a clean damp cloth.

How to truss poultry or game

The purpose of trussing the bird is to keep it a good shape while cooking. Stuffing should be done first.
1 Put the stuffing in the bird at the breast end. If 2 kinds of stuffing are used then 1 kind can be put at the other end. Fold the skin firmly over the back at the neck end.
2 Press the legs down firmly at the sides of the bird.
3 Put a skewer right through the bird, just under the thighs. Turn the bird over and pinion the wings with the skewer. Pass string under the ends of the skewer and cross over at the back. Turn the bird over and tie the string round the tail, securing the ends of the legs.
The bird is now ready to be prepared for cooking and the breast should be well covered with fat or bacon when this is available.

Roasting of poultry with traditional accompaniments

Roast chicken
1 First prepare and stuff bird.
2 With a large bird you can use veal stuffing at one end and a forcemeat stuffing, as with turkey, at the other.
3 With a small chicken where one is using one kind of stuffing put this at the neck, as well as in the body cavity.
4 Small spring chickens when roasted are not stuffed.
5 When ready to roast, chicken should either be covered with fat bacon or with fat of some kind, as it is very important for the breast to be kept really moist.
6 If wished you can turn the bird during cooking so that the breast is downwards and is thus automatically basted by fat from the legs.
7 Do not over-cook. Check correct timing in cooking guide on page 41.
8 If roasting a small spring chicken cover with a generous amount of butter or fat during cooking, as there is no fat on a very young bird.

Spit roasted chickens
The modern spit is ideal for young chickens. Brush with oil or melted fat, put on to the spit and to give a very moist bird brush once or twice during the cooking.
Accompaniments. Bread sauce, bacon rolls, tomatoes, etc.

Roast duck
1 First prepare and stuff bird.
2 For a young duckling a little melted fat can be put over the bird but with an older duck there is plenty of fat under the skin and this will keep the bird moist.
3 Put in oven. Check timing and temperature on page 41.
4 After duck has been cooking for 30–45 minutes and the skin is beginning to brown take a fine skewer and break the skin at intervals. Be careful not to push the skewer in too far. The purpose of this is to allow the surplus fat to run out and to give you a crisp skin. If the skewer is pushed in too far you will make the fat run into the bird and spoil the texture of the flesh.
5 Serve with apple sauce, or orange salad (see pages 88, 89) or sage and onion stuffing (see page 91).

Roast goose
This is roasted just like duck and since a goose is considered by many people to be too fatty it is important that the skin should be pricked at least once, but preferably twice. Serve with same accompaniments as duck.

Roast guinea fowl
While this is roasted like chicken it is a very dry fleshed bird and must be basted very well indeed. If you are not stuffing it a piece of butter inside is a very good idea.
Serve with same accompaniments as chicken or spring chicken.

Roast turkey
1 First prepare and stuff bird. Use two kinds of stuffing, one in the neck and one in the body.
2 Keep the bird very well covered in fat or cover it with fat and then wrap completely in foil.
3 Roast as on page 41, or use the slow method of roasting (see page 41).
4 For the last 30–40 minutes you can remove the foil to crisp the skin.
5 Serve with such stuffings as veal, chestnut, etc. (see pages 90–91). Garnishes may be bacon rolls, sausages, bread sauce or cranberry sauce (see page 89).

To make gravy for poultry

Since poultry is generally stuffed you serve it with a thickened gravy, following the directions on page 26, but it is advisable to cook the giblets to give you an excellent flavoured stock.

To carve poultry

Chicken
1 A good-sized chicken can be carved into about 6–8 portions. Remove the legs and divide in 2, then cut the breast and wings into 2 or 4 joints.
2 A very small spring chicken is divided in 2 or 4 joints.
3 A very large chicken can be carved like turkey.

Turkey
1 Remove leg on to side of dish or separate dish.
2 Cut long thin slices of breast meat and slices off leg.
3 Serve each portion with both light (breast) and dark (leg) meat.

Duck
Cut into 4 joints. Legs are 1 joint each and the breast and wings another.

Goose
Carve as turkey, giving slices of breast and leg meat.

Pressure cooked poultry and game

Boiling chickens should be given 7 minutes per lb. and casseroled game approximately 15–20 minutes. It is however best in a pressure cooker to joint most poultry which means that the breast could be added a little later if desired.

Boiling chickens

To boil
A chicken cooked in this way will provide an excellent meal.
1 Simmer in salted water.
2 Allow approximately 40–45 minutes per lb.
3 Add herbs and vegetables to taste.
4 When the bird is cooked serve it with a white sauce (see page 90) made half with milk and half with chicken stock.
5 This sauce can be varied by adding chopped hard-boiled eggs, parsley or the finely chopped giblets of the bird.

To steam
You may, however, prefer to steam the bird over boiling water.
1 Season it well.
2 Turn the breast downwards in the steamer, buttering this lightly before you do so.

To roast
1 A boiling chicken *can* be roasted. It must be done very very slowly, allowing about 1 hour per lb. (275°F.—Gas Mark 1).
2 It needs lots of fat to keep it moist.

Fried or grilled chicken

Preparation for frying
The young chickens obtainable today are excellent for frying or grilling.
1 First halve them or cut into 4 neat joints i.e. 2 leg joints and 2 breast and wing.
2 Coat lightly with seasoned flour or with a light coating of flour then beaten egg and breadcrumbs.
3 Or use a batter made as pancake batter (see page 60), but allow only ¼ pint milk.
4 The batter coating is more suitable for deep, rather than shallow, frying.

For shallow frying
1 Cook steadily for 5 minutes in hot fat.
2 Turn and cook for a further 5 minutes.
3 Lower the heat and cook very gently through to the middle.

For deep frying
Allow approximately 10 minutes *steady* cooking in hot fat.

For grilling
1 Brush the bird liberally with melted butter.
2 Brown quickly on both sides under the grill.
3 Turn down the heat and allow the bird to cook gently through to the middle.
4 Total cooking time for jointed grilled chicken, approximately 15 minutes.

Chicken pie

cooking time   45 minutes
plus time for cooking chicken

you will need:

small boiling fowl or ¼ large one (with giblets)	6 oz. short crust pastry (see page 63)
seasoning	2 or 3 rashers bacon or pieces of ham
good pinch mixed herbs	2 hard-boiled eggs little lemon rind

1 First simmer the fowl until just tender.
2 Cook the giblets as well.
3 When cooking, add seasoning, mixed herbs and a little lemon rind.
4 Remove meat from bone and cut into small pieces, or cut into joints and slice breast.
5 Mix the light and dark meat together. Chop the uncooked bacon into small pieces. Slice hard-boiled eggs.
6 The giblets should be mixed with the flesh also.
7 Season well.

8 Put a layer of chicken meat, then egg and bacon, into pie dish, continue until all ingredients are used up.
9 Cover with a scant ½ pint chicken stock, put in pie support.
10 Put on pastry, decorate with leaves and a rose, make slit for steam to escape, glaze pie.
11 Bake for about 45 minutes in centre of oven. Start with hot oven (450°F.—Gas Mark 7) then lower to 375°F.—Gas Mark 4.
12 Serve hot or cold.

Chicken stew

cooking time   2½–3 hours

you will need:

1 boiling chicken	3 tomatoes
½ parsnip	2 onions
4 carrots	small turnip
2 hard-boiled eggs (not essential)	3 rashers streaky bacon
2 oz. margarine	salt
1 oz. flour	pepper
good pinch thyme	1 pint chicken stock

1 Put the chicken into a saucepan with enough water to half cover, a good pinch of salt and pepper and the giblets.
2 Simmer steadily for 1 hour.
3 Remove chicken from the stock, cool slightly, then cut into neat joints.
4 Measure off 1 pint of the chicken stock and keep the rest for soups, etc.
5 Chop the giblets into neat pieces.
6 Heat the margarine in a pan, fry the sliced onions, chopped vegetables and tomatoes until tender.
7 Stir in the flour and cook for a few minutes, then gradually add the chicken stock.
8 Brings this to the boil and cook until thickened.
9 Add plenty of seasoning and the thyme.
10 Arrange the chopped giblets, chopped bacon and joints of chicken in a casserole and pour over the sauce.
11 Cover casserole and bake for 1½–2 hours in the centre of a very moderate oven (350°F.—Gas Mark 3).
Just before serving arrange sliced hard-boiled eggs on top.

Game Cooking Guide

name	important points	accompaniments	cooking time and temperatures
grouse	Roast if young but older birds best casseroled in pies, etc. Must be well hung before cooking.	Redcurrant jelly or bread sauce, game chips, fried crumbs, watercress.	35–55 minutes or approximately 2 hours in casserole.
hare	Excellent roasted when young but if older try in a casserole.	As grouse when roasted.	20 minutes per lb. and 20 minutes over.
leveret	Young hare—as hare.	As hare.	As hare.
partridge	Do not hang too long. 3 days at most. At its best when legs yellow. Roast as on page 45 when young. Can be halved and fried or grilled when very young.	As grouse.	30 minutes.
pheasant	Cook as grouse (see page 45). Can be stuffed if desired and chestnut stuffing is ideal or use sliced fried mushrooms by themselves or mixed with chestnut stuffing (see page 90).	As grouse.	15 minutes per lb. and 15 minutes over.
pigeon	Very cheap and excellent value. Roast if young (see page 45) or cook in casserole or as cutlets.	As grouse.	30 minutes for roasting. 2 hours in casserole.
rabbit	Can be roasted if young—put in pies or in pudding, etc. (see pages 29, 45).	If roasting, sage and onion stuffing (see page 91).	20 minutes per lb. and 20 minutes over for roasting. 1½–2 hours in casserole.

name	important points	accompaniments	cooking time and temperatures
woodcock	Do not draw, as intestines delicious (see below for roasting game). Do put toast underneath. Can be halved and fried.	As grouse	25–30 minutes

Cooking game

Much of the game available can only be obtained for part of the year and it is an offence to kill it during the closed season. Most game is best if hung for several days, an even longer period is prescribed by many people. Do keep it well basted or covered during cooking so the flesh does not dry.

To roast game

1 Cover with plenty of fat bacon or fat.
2 Roast in moderately hot oven (400–425°F.— Gas Mark 5–6).

To casserole game

1 Brown the bird or jointed hare in hot fat.
2 Fry onions, mushrooms and other vegetables in fat.
3 Stir in 2 oz. flour, then cook for a few minutes.
4 Add 1 pint good brown stock, seasoning, little port wine.
5 Cook until thick sauce.
6 Put game and vegetables in casserole. Pour over sauce.
7 Cook for 2–3 hours in covered casserole in very moderate oven.

Roast grouse

1 Cover the grouse with fat bacon or plenty of fat.
2 Roast in a hot oven for the first 15 minutes.
3 If very young birds you can continue roasting in a hot oven for a further 15–20 minutes.
4 If in any doubt as to whether the bird is young and tender lower the heat and allow a good 45 minutes in a just moderate oven.
5 Accompaniments as for all game.

Pigeon cutlets

cooking time   20 minutes

you will need:

2 young pigeons   8 oz. sausage meat
1 egg   1–2 rashers of bacon
breadcrumbs   fat for frying

1 Cut the pigeons into halves, take out as many bones as possible.
2 Cut the rashers of bacon into very small pieces and add to the sausage meat.
3 Divide mixture into 4 and press against each half of the pigeon.
4 Beat the egg, dip the pigeon cutlets into this, then coat with breadcrumbs.
5 Fry the cutlets until crisp and brown on the outside, about 5 minutes either side.
6 Lower the heat and cook gently for 10 minutes.
7 Serve with young carrots and potatoes.

Boiled rabbit

cooking time $1\frac{1}{2}$–$1\frac{3}{4}$ hours

you will need:

1 rabbit   1 oz. flour
about 12 oz. diced   seasoning
   mixed root vegetables chopped parsley
1 pint water   large onion
4 oz. fat bacon $\frac{1}{4}$ pint milk

1 Wash the rabbit in cold water to which a little vinegar has been added, to whiten the flesh.
2 Cut into neat pieces.
3 Dice the bacon and put into the pan with chopped onion, vegetables, rabbit, seasoning and water.
4 Season well, put on the lid and simmer gently for about $1\frac{1}{2}$ hours until the rabbit is tender.
5 Blend the flour with the milk and stir into the liquid.
6 Bring to the boil, stirring well and cook until smooth and thickened.
7 Taste and re-season as necessary.
8 Garnish with chopped parsley.

Creamed rabbit

1 As in preceding recipe but instead of the fat bacon use streaky bacon.
2 Omit root vegetables and use just onion and a few mushrooms.
3 Use a little less water but $1\frac{1}{2}$ gills milk and $\frac{1}{2}$ gill thin cream.

Chapter 7
Main Meal—Vegetables

As well as giving you the way to prepare most of the known vegetables of today you will find quite a number of fairly substantial vegetable dishes that can be served for a light meal by themselves.

Correct cooking of vegetables

1 In order to retain both colour and vitamin content in vegetables it is important to cook them with care.
2 Unless stated to the contrary vegetables should go into a small quantity of boiling salted water.
3 In the case of a large amount of vegetables, like cabbage, they should be added steadily rather than all at once. By putting into the water in this way the liquid keeps boiling.
4 Put a lid onto the pan and try and serve the vegetables immediately they are cooked. Keeping them hot, even for a short time, causes a loss of vitamins.
5 When cooking root vegetables, particularly potatoes, steady cooking, rather than too rapid, is considered advisable.
6 Most vegetables can be cooked with great success in a pressure cooker.

Basic ways of serving vegetables

Artichokes: globe
1 Cook steadily in boiling salted water for about 30 minutes.
2 Serve with a little melted butter or a white, cheese or hollandaise sauce.

Artichokes: Jerusalem
1 Scrub well and peel or scrape.
2 Soak in a little cold water, adding a few drops of vinegar.
3 Cook for about 30 minutes in boiling salted water adding a few drops of vinegar.
4 Serve with melted butter, and a white, cheese or hollandaise sauce.

Asparagus
1 Wash carefully, then cut off a little of the thick white base of stalks.
2 Either steam or boil the bunch in salted water in a tall pan for 20–25 minutes.
3 Serve with melted butter or mousseline sauce.

Beans: broad
1 Shell and wash, unless very young, when they can be cooked whole.
2 Cook in boiling salted water for about 20 minutes.

3 Serve with a little melted butter and chopped parsley.

Beans: French or runner
1 Wash and string.
2 French beans can be left whole, but runner beans are better thinly sliced.
3 Cook steadily in boiling salted water for about 15 minutes.

Beetroot
1 Wash carefully and cook in boiling salted water until soft.
2 Time will vary according to size, but test by pressing gently.
3 Generally served cold with salads, but delicious hot with parsley or hollandaise sauce.

Brussels sprouts
1 Mark across with a sharp knife at base of each sprout.
2 Boil rapidly like cabbage.

Cabbage: spring, summer or Savoy
1 Shred finely with sharp knife.
2 Boil rapidly for about 10 minutes in salted water.
3 Serve raw in salads.

Carrots
1 Scrub well or scrape.
2 Cook in boiling salted water until soft.

Cauliflower
1 Cut off thick stalks and outer leaves, divide heart into small sprigs.
2 Cook rapidly in boiling salted water.
3 Serve with white, parsley or cheese sauce.

Celery, celeriac and chicory
1 Generally eaten raw and in salads, but very good cooked.
2 Divide into neat pieces.
3 Cook in boiling salted water for about 20 minutes.
4 Serve with white, parsley or cheese sauce.

Corn on the cob
1 Wash corn cob, strip off outer green leaves.
2 Boil in salted water for about 20 minutes, until the corn feels soft.
3 Serve with a little melted butter.
4 Do not boil too quickly or for too long, otherwise the corn becomes tough again.

Cucumber
1 Generally served raw with vinegar.
2 Can be boiled in pieces in salted water or braised as celery.

Eggplant or aubergine
1 Wash and remove any hard stalk.
2 Bake in a casserole with knob of margarine and little milk for 30 minutes.
3 Can be stuffed or fried like potatoes.

Endive
1 Shred and serve in salads.

Fennel
1 A little, cut finely, flavours a salad.
2 It can be cooked like other vegetables, in boiling salted water.
3 If cooked, serve with a white sauce.
4 Particularly good served with fish.

Haricot beans (dried)
1 Dried haricot beans require soaking for 48 hours.
2 Then simmer in the water in which they were soaked, for about 1½ hours.
3 Serve with cheese sauce or include in casserole dishes.

Leeks
1 Cut off roots and outer leaves, split down the middle so they can be thoroughly washed.
2 Use in place of onions in soups and stews.
3 Or boil for 30 minutes in salted water.
4 Serve with white or cheese sauce.

Lettuce
1 Normally served in salads.
2 But can be cooked like cabbage.
3 Or cook in a little butter in a covered pan until soft, or braised.

Mushrooms
1 Can be fried or grilled in butter or baked in a covered casserole for about 30 minutes.
2 Mushrooms can also be stewed in milk, then remaining liquid thickened with a little flour or cornflour.

Onions
1 Put into soups and stews, fried with meat or savoury dishes.
2 As a separate vegetable boil for a good hour in salted water.
3 Serve with white sauce.

Parsnips
1 Put into soups and stews, but do not have too large a proportion of parsnips as their flavour is very strong and will dominate the dish.
2 Very good baked round the meat.

Peas
1 Shell and cook steadily in boiling salted water for 10–15 minutes.
2 Serve with a little melted butter.
3 Mint and a teaspoon of sugar improve the flavour.

Peppers: green
1 Shredded and served in salads.
2 Can be baked and stuffed.

Potatoes
1 Always put into boiling salted water and cook steadily until soft.
2 Can also be fried, roasted, baked in their jackets or steamed.

Salsify
1 Wash or scrape well, then cook as for Jerusalem artichokes.
2 Serve with a little melted butter and chopped parsley.

Spinach
1 Wash leaves in several waters.
2 There is no need to add water to spinach, so just put into a strong pan with a little salt and boil rapidly until tender, about 15 minutes.
3 Either rub through a sieve or turn on to a board and chop finely.
4 Return to the pan with a little milk and butter and re-heat.

Tomatoes
1 Delicious raw, or can be used in every way cooked, they add flavour to all savoury dishes.

Turnips
1 Put into soups and stews.
2 When young they are delicious cooked in boiled salted water, then mashed.

Vegetable marrow
1 Peel, cut into neat pieces.
2 Steam over boiling salted water adding a little salt.
3 Or bake, stuffed.
4 Or boil in salted water until tender.
5 Serve with cheese or white sauce.

New ways with vegetables
Jerusalem artichokes
1 Cook with a little lemon juice in the water to keep them white.

2 Try them in a cheese sauce, topped with breadcrumbs and grated cheese and browned under the grill.

Broad beans
1 When young these can be cooked with their pods as well.
2 Shred the pods like runner beans.
3 Try a hot bean and bacon salad, by mixing the cooked beans with diced crisp bacon and chopped hard-boiled eggs.

Runner beans
1 These are delicious cold in salads.
2 Toss in well-seasoned oil and vinegar.

Beetroot
1 An excellent hot vegetable. Make a creamy thick white sauce, stir in the coarsely shredded cooked beetroot and heat.
2 Or toss the sliced cooked beetroot in a little hot butter and parsley.

Brussels sprouts
1 They have a perfect partner in cooked chestnuts.
2 Drain sprouts, mix with the chestnuts, toss in hot butter.
3 Serve with beef or poultry, particularly good with duck.

Cabbage
1 To give it an entirely different flavour, cover lightly and strain.
2 Then mix with a little chopped cooked bacon, apple and seasoning.

Raw Cabbage
1 An ideal salad base – try it with grated apple, sultanas, and chopped celery.
2 Moisten with mayonnaise or a good French dressing.

Red cabbage
1 A very good cooked vegetable, as well as being the basis of a pickle.
2 Try cooked red cabbage with a few caraway seeds.

Cauliflower
1 Can be served raw in salads.
2 Divide into small flowerets.
3 Roll in thick mayonnaise then in grated cheese and paprika pepper.

Carrots
1 Excellent mashed with a little butter and grated nutmeg.
2 Serve topped with thick gammon rashers and tomatoes.

Celeriac
1 This is a vegetable so often forgotten – looking like a large ugly turnip it tastes just like celery.
2 Dice and cook in boiling salted water, serve with cheese sauce.
3 Or grate and put in salads.

Celery sticks
1 Ideal party fare – cut into short lengths and fill with:
2 Cream cheese and chopped walnuts.
3 Blue cheese mixed with mayonnaise.
4 Grated cheese mixed with chopped apple and mayonnaise.

Cucumbers
1 These can be served hot as well as cold in salads.
2 Peel and cook for about 10–15 minutes in boiling salted water, (depending on thickness of slices).
3 Do not overcook.
4 Drain and serve with melted butter and a white, tomato or cheese sauce (see page 90).
5 Excellent with fish.
6 Or stuff and bake cucumbers just as you do marrows.

Eggplants or aubergines
1 These long purple-coloured vegetables can be sliced thinly and fried.
2 Excellent instead of potatoes with fish.

Leeks
1 Try using them to make a supper savoury.
2 Cook until tender in boiling salted water, drain well.
3 Wrap a slice of cheese (processed ideal) over each cooked leek.
4 Cover with a wide rasher of bacon.
5 Cook steadily under the grill or in the oven.

Peas
1 Delicious cooked the French way.
2 Line a casserole with lettuce leaves and add sliced or small onions, the peas, then butter, seasoning and more damp lettuce leaves.
3 Cover the casserole tightly and cook for about 1 hour in a moderate oven.

Potatoes
1 These can be cooked in so many different ways.
2 *Allumette* or *Matchstick potatoes:*
3 Cut them like matchsticks and fry. Excellent with grills and steaks.
4 Or *Dutch potatoes:*
5 These are made by peeling large potatoes and scoop out hole in centre. Insert a sausage in

this and roast in hot fat. Serve with bacon rashers.

5 *New potatoes:*
7 These can be roasted around the joint. Do not attempt to scrape but scrub, then dry and roast in the usual way.

Swedes

1 Excellent roasted round the joint.
2 Par-boil for about 15 minutes.
3 Drain and roast for about 1–1¼ hours.

Vegetable marrow

1 Try frying or roasting it for a change.

Danish stuffed cabbage

cooking time   1¼–1½ hours
you will need:

8 large cabbage leaves	½ pint brown sauce or can of tomato soup

rice stuffing

2 oz. cooked well-drained rice	1 or 2 hard-boiled chopped eggs
seasoning	1 large skinned and chopped tomato
3 oz. grated cheese	

1 Wash the leaves well and put into boiling salted water for a few minutes only to make them soft and easy to roll.
2 Drain.
3 Blend the ingredients for the stuffing.
4 Put into each leaf, roll firmly and secure with cotton.
5 Put into a casserole.
6 Cover with brown sauce or can of tomato soup.
7 Cover the casserole and cook for almost 1½ hours in a very moderate oven (350°F.—Gas Mark 3).

Stuffed cauliflower

cooking time   20–25 minutes
you will need:

1 large cauliflower	1 gill thick cheese sauce (or 1 gill tomato sauce)
2 or 3 hard-boiled eggs	
few capers	1 tablespoon chopped cucumber or gherkins (this can be omitted)
seasoning	
2 oz. grated cheese	

1 Remove the thick stalks of the cauliflower and cook in rapidly boiling salted water for a few minutes.
2 Add the whole cauliflower and continue cooking until tender but unbroken.
3 Carefully remove the centre of the cauliflower.
4 Chop this finely and mix with the cheese sauce, chopped eggs, cucumber, capers and seasoning.
5 Pile this back in the centre of the cauliflower.
6 Arrange the green stalk-pieces round.
7 Sprinkle the top with grated cheese and brown under a hot grill or in the oven.
8 Serve with crisp toast or creamed potatoes, peas and grilled tomatoes.

Leek and tomato casserole

cooking time   1–1¼ hours
you will need:

8 good-sized leeks	4 large tomatoes
4 large potatoes	seasoning
grated cheese	good knob of butter

1 Wash the leeks and cut into small pieces.
2 Peel and slice the potatoes thinly, skin and slice the tomatoes.
3 Fry the leeks in hot butter until golden coloured then add the tomatoes, potatoes and seasoning.
4 Either put into a covered casserole or put a very tightly fitting lid on the pan.
5 Cook very gently until tender.
6 Serve covered with grated cheese.

Curried lentils

cooking time   1 hour
you will need:

8 oz. lentils	2 oz. dripping or margarine
3 oz. boiled rice	
1 tablespoon curry powder	1 small apple
	1 teaspoon sugar
1 teaspoon jam	good pinch salt and pepper
few drops lemon juice	
2 large onions	

1 Soak the lentils for a few hours and then simmer in the cold water in which they were soaked until just soft.
2 Heat the fat and fry the onion and apple until just soft.
3 Add the curry powder, the lentils and all other ingredients.
4 Heat well, then pour over the boiled rice.

Onion and potato pancakes (with fried eggs)

cooking time   10 minutes
you will need:

4 large potatoes	1 large onion
about 2 oz. flour	4 eggs
fat for frying	seasoning
parsley	

1 Peel and dry the potatoes.
2 Grate very coarsely.
3 Put into a basin with the grated onion, seasoning, a little chopped parsley and enough flour to bind.
4 Heat about 2 oz. fat in a pan.
5 Drop spoonfuls of the potato mixture into the hot fat, flattening each spoonful to make a large round.
6 Fry steadily until golden brown, turn and cook on the second side.
7 Drain, serve with fried eggs. Garnish with parsley.

Onion and mushroom flan

cooking time   40 minutes

you will need:

8-inch flan case made from 5 oz. short crust pastry (see page 63)	6 oz. mushrooms
	6 oz. margarine
2 large, very thinly sliced onions	2 eggs
	2 tablespoons milk
seasoning	2 tablespoons grated cheese

1 Bake the flan case 'blind' for about 10 minutes to 'set' it, but it must not be brown.
2 Keep aside one whole mushroom for garnish.
3 Slice remaining mushrooms and onions, and fry in the hot margarine.
4 Put into the half-baked flan case.
5 Beat the eggs with the milk, add the seasoning and grated cheese.
6 Pour over the onion and mushrooms.
7 Set for about 30 minutes in the centre of a moderate oven (375°F.—Gas Mark 4), when the pastry should be golden brown and the egg mixture firm.

Savoury rice

cooking time   35 minutes

you will need:

8 oz. Patna rice	2 onions
8 oz. tomatoes	4 oz. mushrooms
chopped parsley	salt
cayenne pepper	pepper
2–3 oz. fat for frying	

1 Boil the rice for about 20 minutes in plenty of salted water.
2 Fry the chopped onions until soft.
3 Slice the tomatoes and mushrooms and add these to the onions.
4 Complete the frying and mix in the cooked rice.
5 Season and serve cold or hot sprinkled with parsley.

Devilled tomatoes

cooking time   20 minutes

you will need:

8 medium-sized tomatoes	1 oz. margarine
	2 oz. cooked rice
1 tablespoon chutney	2 eggs
1 teaspoon curry powder	small grated onion

1 Take the tops off the tomatoes.
2 Scoop out the centre pulp.
3 Heat the margarine.
4 Fry the onion until soft.
5 Add all the other ingredients, including the tomato pulp.
6 Season well and cook for a few minutes then pile into the tomatoes.
7 Bake for 15 minutes in a moderately hot oven (400°F.—Gas Mark 5).

Tomato pie

cooking time   50 minutes

you will need:

6 oz. short crust pastry (see page 63)	1 lb. tomatoes
	4 oz. breadcrumbs
3 oz. grated cheese	1 oz. butter
1 onion – lightly fried	seasoning

1 Cut two tomatoes into slices.
2 Heat remainder gently until a pulp.
3 Line a pie dish with the pastry and fill with the tomatoes, mixed with the onion, half the crumbs and half the cheese.
4 Season well.
5 Cover the top with the rest of the crumbs, cheese and butter.
6 Bake for approximately 40 minutes in the centre of a hot oven (450°F.—Gas Mark 7), lowering the heat after 20 minutes.
7 Garnish with sliced tomato.

Vegetable curry

cooking time   50–60 minutes

you will need:

boiled rice	beans, peas, carrots, diced turnips (very few, as they have strong flavour)
1 lb. mixed vegetables which can include	
for the sauce	
2 oz. margarine	1 onion
1 tablespoon curry powder (little less if wished)	1 apple
	1 tablespoon flour
	1 dessertspoon desiccated coconut
1 tablespoon dried fruit	
1 teaspoon sugar	seasoning
1 dessertspoon chutney	1 pint water or stock
squeeze of lemon juice	

1 Heat the margarine.
2 Fry the onion and apple until soft.
3 Add the curry powder and flour.
4 Cook for several minutes.
5 Add the liquid.
6 Bring to the boil.
7 Stir in all the other ingredients for sauce.
8 Add the diced vegetables (these should be fairly large pieces) and simmer for about 35 minutes or longer.
9 Serve in a border of boiled rice.

Vegetable stew with cheese dumplings

cooking time   40 minutes

you will need:

8 medium-sized potatoes	4 oz. grated cheese
	8 small onions
4 leeks	8 carrots
head celery	seasoning
chopped parsley	dumplings (see page 30)

1 Cook the vegetables in boiling water, until almost soft.
2 Make the dumplings, adding the cheese to the mixture before making moist.

Put into the vegetable water and cook for approximately 15–20 minutes.
Lift vegetables and dumplings out of liquid into hot dish and use the stock to make either a brown or white sauce.

Vegetable pie

cooking time   30 minutes

you will need:

½ pint cheese sauce (see page 90)

1 lb. mixed cooked root vegetables

knob margarine

little grated cheese

1 lb. creamed potatoes

Drain vegetables, dice and mix with sauce.
Place in a pie dish.
Cover with creamed potatoes.

4 Put knob of margarine on top and a little grated cheese.
5 Bake for 25–30 minutes in a moderately hot oven (400°F.—Gas Mark 5).

Vegetable pudding

cooking time   3–4 hours

you will need:

8 oz. suet crust pastry (see page 64)

for the filling

½ swede

2 tomatoes

stock

a little chopped parsley

1 medium-sized turnip

2 onions

2 oz. soaked and cooked butter beans

4 good-sized carrots

As for steak and kidney pudding (see page 37), dicing all the vegetables into small cubes.

Chapter 8

Main Meal—Family Puddings (cold)

Cold sweets are particularly tempting in summer weather or after a heavy main course. In the following chapter you will find some excellent recipes for a variety of cold sweets.

Apple ginger tartlets

cooking time   12 minutes

you will need:

6 oz. short crust pastry (see page 63)

1 tablespoon apricot jam

2 tablespoons finely chopped crystallized ginger (if preferred,

sultanas or well drained chopped pineapple could be used instead)

5 oz. thick, sweetened apple pulp

1 gill thick custard or

1 gill whipped cream

to decorate

sieved icing sugar

angelica

glacé cherries

pieces of ginger

Line 12 deep patty tins with a thin layer of the short crust pastry.
Bake for about 12 minutes near the top of a hot oven (425–450°F.—Gas Mark 6–7) until the pastry is golden brown and firm.
Cool, then put in a little jam, then the filling. To make this, mix the apple pulp with the ginger and cream or custard.
Dust the top of the tarts with sugar and put a cherry and angelica or piece of ginger in the centre of each tart.

Apple ginger flan

cooking time   20–25 minutes

Use above recipe but bake the pastry in an

8-inch flan case, serve with a border of piped cream, and stand tiny shapes of baked pastry on this.

Apricot fluff

cooking time   10 minutes in pressure cooker or 1 hour

you will need:

8 oz. dried apricots

2 eggs

3 oz. sugar

water

1 lemon jelly

1 can evaporated milk

few chopped nuts

1 Soak the dried apricots overnight in enough water to cover.
2 Simmer or cook in pressure cooker until tender, adding sugar to taste.
3 Sieve or beat until smooth, removing a few for decoration.
4 Measure this pulp and add enough water to give ¼ pint, dissolve the jelly in this while very hot.
5 Cool, then pour onto the egg yolks and evaporated milk stirring all together.
6 Allow to stiffen and fold in the stiffly beaten egg white.
7 Taste and add more sugar if wished.
8 Pour into 6 glasses and decorate with the apricots and a few chopped nuts if wished.

Apricot pie

you will need:

can apricots or 8 oz. cooked fresh apricots	$\frac{3}{4}$ pint water lemon jelly
about 18 sponge finger biscuits	2 eggs 1 gill cream

1 Strain off syrup from the apricots and dip the biscuits in this.
2 Line the bottom of an attractive pie plate or dish with some of the biscuits.
3 Halve the rest and use to line the sides of the dish.
4 Make sure the biscuits are dipped very quickly in and out of the syrup so they do not become soggy.
5 Make the lemon jelly with $\frac{3}{4}$ pint water only, pour on to the egg yolks and whisk sharply together.
6 When the jelly begins to set add the chopped apricots and stiffly beaten egg whites.
7 Pour into the sponge finger case.
8 When set decorate with the lightly whipped cream and a few apricot halves too, if any are left.

Apple mousse

cooking time	few minutes plus time to cook apples

you will need:

1 pint thick apple purée	glacé cherries 3 eggs
2 level teaspoons powder gelatine	1 tablespoon lemon juice
2 or 3 ginger nut biscuits for decoration	$\frac{1}{2}$ gill water sugar

1 Separate the eggs.
2 Stir the beaten egg yolks into the apple purée together with the powder gelatine, dissolved in the very hot water and lemon juice.
3 When just beginning to stiffen fold in the stiffly beaten egg whites and sugar to taste.
4 Pile into 6 glasses and decorate each with a cherry and a border of fine ginger nut crumbs.

Apple and lemon mousse—Cook apples with lemon rind. Use $\frac{1}{2}$ gill lemon juice instead of water.
Hawaiian mousse—Use half apple purée and half chopped pineapple.
Apple ginger mousse.—Add little powdered ginger to the apple and chopped crystallised ginger.

Caramel custard

cooking time	$2\frac{1}{2}$ hours

you will need:

for the caramel

3 oz. loaf or granulated sugar	4 tablespoons water

for the custard

3 eggs or 4 egg yolks	$\frac{1}{2}$ oz. margarine or butter
1 dessertspoon sugar	
1 pint milk	

1 First make the caramel. Put the sugar and half the water into a small strong saucepan.
2 Stir over a low heat until you can no longer feel the grittiness of the sugar on the bottom of the pan, it is then dissolved.
3 Boil steadily, without stirring, until it turns dark brown.
4 Watch during this process for it soon turns black and burns.
5 Take the pan off the heat, then add the rest of the water.
6 When you do this the caramel will become a sticky ball, but return to the heat, stir gently and it will soon become liquid again.
7 Grease a mould with the margarine or butter.
8 If using a metal mould you can safely pour in the caramel sauce while very hot.
9 With a china or glass mould or basin it must cool slightly.
10 Wait until the caramel sauce is cold before adding the custard.
11 To make the custard: Pour hot, but not boiling milk on to the eggs beaten with the sugar. Strain over the caramel; this is not essential, but it ensures you have no small pieces of egg floating on top.
12 Half fill a dish, slightly larger than the basin or mould, with cold water.
13 Stand the mould in this and bake for about $2\frac{1}{2}$ hours in the centre of a very moderate oven (275–300°F.—Gas Mark 2) until firm or steam over hot water.
14 Too great a heat causes curdling and this spoils the custard.
15 Cool the caramel custard and when nearly cold turn out on to a dish.
16 Do not wait until it is quite cold otherwise some of the caramel will stick to the mould.

Compote of fruit

This is a word used to describe cooked fruit but the fruit must be left in good sized pieces and not over-cooked. It can consist of a mixture of fresh and dried fruits cooked separately and mixed.

Custard and fruit mould

cooking time	10 minutes

you will need:

1 fruit-flavoured jelly	1 pint custard sauce, well sweetened (see page 64)
1 gill well-drained chopped fruit	some whole fruit to decorate
scant $\frac{1}{2}$ pint water	

Dissolve jelly in just under ½ pint very hot water.
2 Stir into custard and when cool add fruit.
3 Pour into rinsed mould.
4 Turn out and when firm decorate with whole fruit, etc.

Fruit creams

cooking time   5–10 minutes

you will need:

1 fruit flavoured jelly	5 oz. thick fruit pulp
1 gill thick cream or	(choose fruit which will
custard or evaporated	mix well with jelly)
milk	fruit and nuts (to
	decorate)

1 Stir jelly into just under ¾ pint of very hot water.
2 When dissolved add fruit pulp.
3 Cool, then add cream or custard or evaporated milk.
4 Pour into glasses or a large dish and decorate with fruit, nuts, etc.

Fruit flan

cooking time   20–25 minutes

you will need:

5 oz. short or flan	any mixture of canned or
pastry (see page 63)	fresh fruit, i.e. mandarin
	oranges, bananas,
	cherries, peaches

1 Bake the pastry flan 'blind'.
2 Drain fruit carefully and arrange in the cold flan.
3 For a 7-inch flan, blend 1 rounded teaspoon arrowroot with 1 gill fruit syrup.
4 Boil until thick and clear then add a few drops of colouring if wished.
5 Allow syrup to cool but pour it over the fruit before it becomes too thick.

Fruit salads

There are many ways of making a good fruit salad. The quickest and easiest are as follows:

Fruit salad with canned fruit

1 Open a can of some fruit that is not available, or in season, i.e. pineapple, peaches, apricots.
2 Slice or dice the fruit and then add your fresh fruit to it.
3 Grapes should be pipped and some people like them skinned.
4 Apples should be added at the end of the preparations to keep them as crisp as possible. Slice thinly.
5 Bananas should be well covered in the syrup to keep them a good colour.
6 Oranges. To avoid adding pips, pith, skins, etc. to the salad, peel the orange with a knife but

as you do this cut into fruit very slightly so removing any of the outside pith. With the sharp knife cut slices of orange between the skin.

Fresh fruit salad

1 Boil sugar and water to give the syrup, allowing 4–8 oz. to each pint of water.
2 Add lemon or orange juice to flavour.
3 Add this to the fruit.
4 For special occasions a little sherry, kirsch, cherry or apricot brandy can be added.
5 If no syrup is required the diced fruit should just be mixed together and moistened with the juice of an orange.

To stew fruit

The method used depends on the type of fruit.

For hard fruit

1 Put into a pan with sugar and water, the amount of water depending on how much syrup is required.
2 Simmer gently.

For very delicate fruit (i.e. soft fruit, forced rhubarb, etc.).

1 Put the fruit in a basin over hot water.
2 Add sugar and little, if any, water.
3 Cook very gently.

To poach fruit

Where it is important to keep the shape of fruit the best method is as follows:

1 Prepare the syrup.
2 When this is really hot, put in the fruit.
3 Soft fruits will not need any cooking, but should just stand in the hot syrup as it cools.
4 Other fruit should be cooked very gently in the syrup.

Fruit fool

1 Blend quantities of a very thick fruit purée with a thick custard.
2 For special occasions, use whipped cream instead of custard.
3 Suitable fruits: gooseberry, plum.
4 When cooking the fruit use the minimum amount of water.
5 The blended mixture should be put in tall glasses.
6 Top with cream and whole fruit.

Fruit jellies

To mould in layers

1 Pour a small amount of the cool jelly into a mould.
2 Allow this to set lightly.

3 Arrange some of the fruit on top.
4 Pour over liquid jelly.
5 Leave until firm.
6 Continue filling the mould like this.

Fruit whip

cooking time   5–15 minutes

you will need:

1 lb. fruit*	1 gill water
3 oz. sugar (or to taste)	juice and finely grated rind of 1 large lemon
3 egg whites	2 teaspoons powdered gelatine

*Rhubarb, black or red currants, raspberries, gooseberries, plums are ideal for this sweet.

1 Cut the fruit into small pieces.
2 Put into a pan with half the water, lemon rind, juice and sugar.
3 Cook until a smooth pulp.
4 This can be sieved but really is unnecessary.
5 Dissolve the gelatine in the remaining $\frac{1}{2}$ gill of very hot water.
6 Stir into the fruit pulp.
7 Continue stirring until thoroughly dissolved.
8 Allow to cool and begin to stiffen then fold in the stiffly beaten egg whites.
9 Pile into 4 or 5 glasses.

Lemon honeycomb mould

cooking time   5 minutes

you will need:

1 gill lemon juice	$\frac{3}{4}$ pint water
$\frac{1}{2}$ oz. powdered gelatine	1 large fresh egg
	2 oz. sugar

1 Put the lemon juice, water, sugar and egg yolk into a saucepan.
2 Heat well for about 5 minutes (without boiling) until very slightly thickened.
3 Remove from the heat and cool slightly.
4 Soften the powder gelatine in 2 tablespoons of cold water, pour on the lemon mixture.
5 When this is quite cold fold in the stiffly beaten egg white.
6 Pour into a rinsed mould to set.

Mocha flan

cooking time   25 minutes

you will need:

4–5 oz. short or sweet crust pastry (see page 63)	1 gill coffee
$\frac{3}{4}$ pint milk	1 packet chocolate blancmange powder
2 oz. sugar	1 orange and orange rind

1 Roll out the pastry.
2 Line a flan case and bake 'blind' in a hot oven (425–450°F.—Gas Mark 6–7) until crisp and golden brown.
3 Meanwhile prepare the filling. Blend the blancmange powder with the cold coffee.

4 Bring the milk to the boil, pour over the chocolate mixture.
5 Return to the pan with sugar and grated rind of the orange.
6 Cook until very smooth and thick.
7 Pour into the flan case.
8 Decorate with skinned sections of orange and serve at once.

Mock cream

cooking time   5 minutes

you will need:

1–2 oz. margarine or butter (if you can use butter it makes a very much better cream)	1 tablespoon cornflour
	1 gill milk
	1 oz. castor sugar

1 Blend the cornflour to a smooth mixture with the milk.
2 Put into a saucepan and bring slowly to the boil, stirring all the time.
3 Cook until thick. Allow to become quite cold.
4 Cream the margarine or butter and sugar until very soft.
5 On no account warm the fat. *Gradually* beat in spoonfuls of the cornflour mixture.
6 The more you beat this the better it becomes.

Sponge flan

cooking time   12 minutes

you will need:

2 eggs	2 oz. sugar
2 oz. flour	
filling	
canned or cooked fruit	1 good teaspoon
cream to decorate	arrowroot or powdered
1 gill strained fruit syrup	gelatine

1 Make the sponge mixture by the whisking method as in sponge sandwich (see page 79).
2 Put it into a well greased and floured flan tin.
3 Bake for approximately 12 minutes in a moderately hot oven (400°F.—Gas Mark 5).
4 Turn out carefully and allow to cool.
5 Arrange the cold, well drained fruit in this.
6 Blend the syrup with the arrowroot.
7 Cook until thick and clear.
8 Cool slightly and then cover the fruit with this.
9 Decorate with cream.
10 If using gelatine you must dissolve this in the hot syrup then wait until just beginning to set.

Trifle

cooking time   depending on ingredients used

There are many ways of making a trifle. Below you will find both simple and more elaborate methods.

Simple methods

1 Split sponge cakes and spread with jam.

Put at the bottom of the dish.

Pour over the sponge cakes hot custard and decorate with a little cream, glacé cherries, etc.

With jelly

Many people prefer jelly used with the custard.

Pour hot jelly over the sponge cakes.

When set top with a layer of custard, which should of course be cool or the jelly will melt. Decorate with cream, cherries, etc.

For richer trifle

1 Soak sponge cakes in sherry.
2 Or if this is not desired, use a fruit purée or canned fruit.
3 Over that sprinkle chopped almonds.
4 Add either jelly and custard or custard alone.
5 For a very special occasion, top with a thick layer of whipped cream.
6 Decorate with cream, tiny ratafia biscuits, nuts, etc.

Chapter 9

Main Meal—Family Puddings (hot) including Pastry Making and Sweet Sauces

There is nothing more satisfying to end a meal than a delicious hot pudding or flaky pie. Here are a number of recipes for family puddings and pies, both familiar and unusual. At the end of this chapter you will also find a good selection of sweet sauces which can do so much to make a pudding a success.

Apple and orange charlotte

cooking time   30 minutes

you will need:

12 oz. sliced apples	2 oranges
4 oz. breadcrumbs	sugar
2 oz. margarine or butter	water

1 Grate the rind from the oranges.
2 Mix the rind with the breadcrumbs.
3 Put the apples into a saucepan with a little sugar and water and stew until soft.
4 Put half the margarine at the bottom of a pie dish and put into the oven to melt.
5 Press a layer of crumbs on top of the margarine, then a layer of apple pulp and pieces of orange, removing as much of the pith and skin from the orange as possible.
6 Follow with a layer of crumbs.
7 Then the fruit again and a final layer of crumbs.
8 Put the rest of the margarine on top, then a sprinkling of sugar.
9 Bake in the centre of a moderately hot oven (400°F.—Gas Mark 5) for 30 minutes.

Baked jam roly poly

cooking time   55 minutes

you will need:

8 oz. jam	8 oz. suet crust pastry (see page 64)

1 Roll out pastry into a neat oblong about $\frac{1}{4}$ inch thick.
2 Spread with jam.
3 Turn in the ends to prevent jam boiling out and then roll like a Swiss roll.
4 Do this lightly to give room for pastry to rise.
5 Put on to greased tray.
6 Bake in centre of moderately hot oven (425°F. —Gas Mark 6) for about 30 minutes.
7 Lower heat for a further 25 minutes to make sure pastry is cooked.

Blackberry and sponge pudding

cooking time $1\frac{1}{4}$–$1\frac{1}{2}$ hours

you will need:

3 oz. margarine	3 oz. castor sugar
1 egg	3 oz. self-raising flour
1 oz. breadcrumbs	1 tablespoon milk

topping

8 oz. cooking apples	water
1 rounded teaspoon arrowroot	4–6 oz. blackberries
	3 oz. granulated sugar

1 Cream the margarine and sugar together until very light.
2 Beat in the egg.
3 Fold in the sieved flour and the breadcrumbs.
4 Add milk.
5 Place in a 1-pint pudding basin brushed inside with melted margarine.
6 Cover the basin with double greaseproof paper.

7 Place in a steamer or saucepan with fast boiling water.
8 Cover tightly and steam for $1\frac{1}{4}$–$1\frac{1}{2}$ hours.
9 Peel, core and slice the apples.
10 Place them in a saucepan with $1\frac{1}{2}$ oz. sugar and 1 tablespoon water and cook gently until tender (but do no pulp them).
11 Cook the blackberries in another saucepan with $1\frac{1}{2}$ oz. sugar and 1 gill water.
12 Turn out the pudding on to a heated plate.
13 Strain the juice from the blackberries.
14 Place the blackberries and apples round the pudding.
15 Make the juice up to $\frac{1}{2}$ pint with water.
16 Blend the arrowroot with a little juice.
17 Bring the remainder to the boil in a saucepan.
18 Pour over the mixture stirring all the time.
19 Return to the pan.
20 Bring to the boil and cook gently for 2–3 minutes.
21 Pour into a jug and serve with the pudding.

Caramel pudding

cooking time $1\frac{1}{2}$ hours plus time for making caramel

you will need:

2 oz. sultanas	4 oz. castor sugar
3 egg yolks (use whites for meringues)	2 large slices of stale bread about $\frac{1}{2}$ inch thick
water	
cream (optional)	$\frac{3}{4}$ pint milk

1 Put 3 oz. of sugar and 3 tablespoons water into a pan.
2 Stir until sugar has dissolved.
3 Boil steadily until brown.
4 Add milk, then heat gently until the caramel has dissolved in the milk.
5 Remove crusts from bread.
6 Cut into neat dice and pour caramel-flavoured milk over this.
7 Add rest of sugar, beaten with egg yolks, then sultanas.
8 Leave to stand for 30 minutes.
9 Stir briskly.
10 Pour into greased soufflé dish or basin.
11 Cover with greased paper and steam gently for about $1\frac{1}{2}$ hours until firm.
12 Serve hot or cold, turning out and decorating with glacé cherries and cream, if liked.

Coconut pudding

cooking time $1\frac{1}{4}$ hours

you will need:

approx. 3 oz. dried stale bread	$\frac{1}{2}$ pint milk
lemon-flavoured custard	2–3 oz. sugar
3 oz. desiccated coconut	2 eggs
	grated rind of lemon

1 Heat milk and pour over bread.
2 Add the coconut, sugar and lemon rind.
3 Allow to stand for about 20 minutes.
4 Stir in the very well-beaten eggs at the end of this time.
5 Pour into a greased basin and steam steadily for approximately $1\frac{1}{4}$ hours.
6 Turn out and serve with lemon-flavoured custard.
7 Do not let this pudding boil rapidly otherwise it will curdle.

Chocolate queen of puddings

cooking time   1 hour

you will need:

1 oz. breadcrumbs	1 oz. chocolate powder
2 eggs	2 tablespoons apricot jam
$\frac{1}{2}$ pint milk	3 tablespoons sugar
$\frac{1}{2}$ oz. margarine	

1 Spread half the jam thinly on the bottom of a greased pie dish.
2 Put the crumbs, chocolate powder, milk, margarine and 1 tablespoon sugar into a saucepan.
3 Heat gently.
4 Separate eggs, then stir in beaten egg yolks.
5 Pour into the pie dish and bake for 20 minutes in centre of moderate oven (375°F.—Gas Mark 4) until pudding feels fairly firm.
6 Spread top with remaining jam.
7 Beat egg whites until stiff, fold in nearly all the sugar.
8 Pile on top of pudding, dusting with remaining sugar.
9 Bake in a very slow oven (275°F.—Gas Mark 1) for about 40 minutes until meringue is firm.

Coffee fudge pudding

cooking time   45 minutes

you will need:

2 oz. margarine	2 oz. sugar
4 oz. flour (if plain flour use $1\frac{1}{2}$ level teaspoons baking powder)	2 eggs
	4 oz. coffee fudge
	2 level tablespoons castor sugar

1 Cream together margarine and 2 oz. sugar.
2 Separate eggs, add egg yolks, flour and fudge cut into small pieces. Mix well.
3 Put into greased pie dish.
4 Bake for approximately 40–45 minutes in centre of moderate oven (375°F.—Gas Mark 4).
5 Whisk the whites of eggs, fold in 2 level tablespoons sugar.
6 Pile on the pudding and set in the oven to brown lightly.

Vanilla or chocolate fudge can be used instead of coffee fudge.

Danish apple pudding

cooking time   45 minutes

you will need:

8 oz. stale breadcrumbs	1 lb. thick sweetened
4 oz. brown sugar	apple purée (or try
very little lemon (or	thick rhubarb purée
orange) juice	instead)
mixed spice to taste	grated rind of lemon (or
4 oz. margarine	orange

Heat margarine in frying pan and toss crumbs in this until crisp and golden brown, adding sugar and a little spice too if wished.
Mix lemon rind and juice with apple purée.
Grease a dish and fill with alternate layers of crumbs and apple, beginning and ending with crumbs.
Bake for about 45 minutes in centre of very moderate oven (350°F.—Gas Mark 3).

Date and apple turnovers

cooking time   20–30 minutes

you will need:

4 oz. plain flour	2 oz. cornflour
3 oz. butter or	1 teaspoon castor sugar
margarine	1 egg yolk

1 Sieve the flour and cornflour together.
2 Rub in the butter or margarine.
3 Add the castor sugar.
4 Mix to stiff dough with egg yolk.
5 Roll the pastry thinly and cut into strips approximately 4 inches wide and 8 inches long.

filling

12 oz. cooking apples	4 oz. dates (use cheap
sugar to taste	cooking dates)
	little grated lemon rind

1 Peel, core and slice apples thinly.
2 Stone and chop the dates.
3 Put into a basin with sugar (approximately 2–3 tablespoons) and add lemon rind.
4 Put some of the apple mixture on each piece of pastry.
5 Dampen the edges and fold over to form a square.
6 Press the edges well together and mark with a fork.
7 Put on a baking tray, bake about 20–30 minutes in a fairly hot oven (425°F.—Gas Mark 6).

Date bows

cooking time   20–25 minutes

you will need:

8 oz. short crust pastry	(see page 63)
filling	
1 oz. chopped nuts	4 oz. dates
grated rind and juice	little milk and sugar to
of 1 orange	glaze

1 Roll pastry out 12 inches square.
2 Put filling into saucepan and cook until the dates are jam consistency (5–8 minutes).
3 Cool. Spread the cold date filling over half the pastry.
4 Fold over the other half to form a sandwich.
5 Cut into 4 x 1 inch strips with a knife.
6 Twist in the centre to form a bow.
7 Place on an ungreased baking sheet. Brush with milk and sprinkle with a little sugar.
8 Bake near top of a moderately hot oven (425°F.—Gas Mark 6) for 12–15 minutes.

Egg custards

cooking time   1–2 hours

you will need:

for a lightly set custard

2 eggs*	1 pint milk
1 tablespoon sugar	

for a firm custard

3–4 eggs*	1 pint milk
1 tablespoon sugar	

* Egg yolks only can be used which does give a creamier and better result.

To bake
1 Whisk the eggs with the sugar.
2 Pour over the milk then strain into a buttered dish.
3 Stand the dish in another of cold water. This is to prevent it from curdling.
4 Cook for 1–2 hours in a very slow oven 275°F.—Gas Mark 1) until quite firm.

To steam
1 Put the dish in a steamer covered with buttered paper.
2 The water underneath must never boil. It should be sufficiently cool that you can just bear your finger in it.
3 Steaming will take approximately 2 hours.
Note: Custards can be topped with grated nutmeg before cooking or flavoured with a little chocolate, coffee essence, etc.

Fruit plate pies

Follow directions for rhubarb and date pie – (see page 60) but try these variations:
1 **Apple**—Slice apples, arrange on the pastry sprinkling with sugar, powdered cloves or cinnamon. Use no water.
2 **Apple and sultana**—Add sultanas, grated lemon rind, to sliced fruit.
3 **Blackcurrants**—No water but plenty of sugar with the fruit.
4 **Cherry**—Add very little water and brown sugar for a rich flavour.
5 **Damson and apple**—Use equal quantities of sliced apple and damsons and plenty of sugar.

6 Gooseberry—Top and tail fruit—use fairly green gooseberries for good flavour and plenty of sugar.

7 Mincemeat—Use half canned pineapple or sliced raw apples and half mincemeat. This is a pleasant change from all mincemeat.

Hot fruit trifle

cooking time   approximately 35 minutes

you will need:

4 small sponge cakes	1 can fruit (or 8–12 oz.
3 level tablespoons	stewed fruit)
custard powder	1 pint milk
2 egg whites	3 level tablespoons sugar
	4 oz. castor sugar

1 Cut the sponge cakes in half horizontally and line the base of a fireproof dish.
2 Drain the fruit and pour the juice over the sponge cakes.
3 Cover with the fruit.
4 Blend the custard powder with 2 tablespoons milk taken from the pint, boil the remainder with the 3 tablespoons sugar.
5 Re-stir paste and while milk is still thoroughly boiling pour over the blended powder.
6 Return to the saucepan and boil 1 minute.
7 When slightly cooled, pour over the fruit and sponge cakes and leave for 5 minutes.
8 Whisk the egg whites until stiff, add 1 oz. castor sugar, whisk again and fold in the remainder of the castor sugar. Pile on top of the custard in rough heaps.
9 Bake in a slow oven (300°F.—Gas Mark 2) for 25–30 minutes until the meringue topping is crisp and golden brown.

Jamaican puffs

cooking time   5 minutes

you will need:

6–8 oz. puff pastry (see	4 firm bananas
page 64) or 1 carton	little lemon juice
frozen puff pastry	deep fat for frying
castor sugar	

1 If using frozen puff pastry allow this to stand until just thawed.
2 Roll out the pastry to an oblong approximately 12 inches x 9 inches and trim off the edges.
3 Cut into 8 equal lengths, 1 inch wide, and damp each lightly with water.
4 Peel the bananas, cut across in half and dip in the lemon juice to prevent discoloration.
5 Wind a strip of pastry round each piece of banana to enclose it completely and seal the ends.
6 Fry in hot fat for 4–5 minutes until golden brown.
7 Drain and roll in castor sugar before serving.

Lemon meringue pie (with uncooked filling)

cooking time   from 20 minutes to 2 hours
(see below)

you will need:

1 large can full cream	2 level teaspoons cream
condensed milk	of tartar
juice and grated rind	6 oz. short or flan pastry
1 lemon	(see page 63)
2 eggs	cherries to decorate
2 oz. castor sugar	

1 Roll out pastry, line an 8- or 9-inch flan ring and bake 'blind'.
2 Mix together the full cream condensed milk and lemon juice and rind with the egg yolks and cream of tartar.
3 Pour this mixture into the baked pastry case.
4 Beat the egg whites stiffly, fold in half the sugar, whisk and pile or pipe it on top of flan.
5 Sprinkle with rest of sugar and decorate with cherries.
6 Bake until set in a cool oven (200°F.—Gas Mark ¼ for ½-2 hours to dry the meringue.
7 For immediate serving bake in a moderate oven (375°F.—Gas Mark 4) until golden.
8 If wished put filling into small tartlet cases instead.

Lemon meringue pie (with cooked filling)

cooking time   35–45 minutes

you will need:

6 oz. short crust pastry	1 oz. butter
(see page 63)	grated rind and juice
4 level tablespoons	2 lemons
cornflour	8 oz. castor sugar
½ pint water	2 eggs

1 Make the pastry and roll out on a lightly floured board to the shape and size required.
2 Prepare and bake 'blind' in a deep 7-inch flan case and leave to cool.
3 Blend the cornflour to a smooth paste with a little of the cold water.
4 Bring the butter and rest of the water to the boil, pour over the blended cornflour, stirring all the time. **Return to the heat and cook until thickened.**
5 Remove from the heat and stir in the lemon rind and juice and 4 oz. of the sugar.
6 **Separate the egg** yolks **from the whites.**
7 Stir the yolks into the cooled mixture and pour into the flan case.
8 Whisk the egg whites very stiffly, add 2 oz. sugar and again whisk stiffly.
9 Fold in the remaining 2 oz. sugar.
10 Pile on top of the lemon mixture, making sure that the meringue touches the edge of the pastry all round.

1 Place in the middle of a slow oven (300°F.—Gas Mark 2) for 20–30 minutes or until the meringue is firm and only lightly browned.

2 If serving cold then bake pie for about 45 minutes in a cool oven to make sure meringue is really firm.

Lemon pudding

cooking time   2½ hours

you will need:

2 or 3 large lemons	suet crust pastry (see
3 oz. sugar	page 64)
2 oz. butter	

1 Line basin with suet crust.

2 Halve 2 or 3 large lemons, remove the pips, add butter and sugar.

3 Cover with 'lid' of pastry and steam for about 2¼ hours.

4 When cooked the pudding will be full of a delicious lemon curd.

Norfolk treacle tart

cooking time   30 minutes

you will need:

5 oz. short crust pastry	2 tablespoons cream
(see page 63)	(you can use cream
grated rind of 1 small	from top of milk)
lemon	4 good tablespoons
1 egg	golden syrup
1 oz. margarine	1 teaspoon lemon juice

1 Line a large deep pie plate or flan ring with the pastry and make a decorated edge.

2 Melt the golden syrup with the margarine, grated lemon rind and juice.

3 Cool.

4 Add the cream and beaten egg.

5 Pour into the pastry.

6 Bake in the centre of a moderately hot oven (400°F.—Gas Mark 5) for about 25–30 minutes until pastry is golden brown and the filling firm.

Nutty bread and butter pudding

cooking time   40–50 minutes

you will need:

4 large slices of bread	2½ oz. mixed dried fruit
and butter	2 eggs
2½ oz. chopped nuts	¾ pint milk
1–2 oz. sugar	
for the topping	
1 tablespoon brown	2 tablespoons chopped
sugar	nuts
1 oz. butter	

1 Remove crusts from the bread and butter and arrange in a pie dish so the slices overlap neatly.

2 Whisk eggs and sugar together, add the milk, which should be hot (straining if necessary).

3 Pour over the bread and butter.

4 Add the fruit and nuts.

5 Bake for about 45 minutes in the centre of a very moderate oven (350°F.—Gas Mark 3) until firm.

6 Sprinkle the brown sugar, nuts and butter over the top.

7 Put for a few minutes under a moderately hot grill.

Orange bread and butter pudding

cooking time   45 minutes

you will need:

3 slices bread and	2 tablespoons sultanas
butter, cut thinly from	(not essential)
a large loaf	2 tablespoons crystallized
1 good tablespoon	orange peel
sugar	2 tablespoons finely grated
1 egg	fresh orange peel
	½ pint milk

1 Divide bread and butter into neat triangles, then arrange in greased pie dish.

2 Beat the egg and pour warmed milk over it.

3 Add half the sugar, then the orange peel and sultanas (if being used).

4 Pour over bread and butter and dust top with remaining sugar.

5 Cook for about 45 minutes in a very moderate oven (350°F.—Gas Mark 3)

6 The custard around should be set.

7 For the last 15 minutes move dish to top of oven so that pudding browns and becomes crisp.

Orange queen of puddings

cooking time   1 hour 5 minutes

you will need:

small can mandarin	approximately 2
oranges	tablespoons orange
2 large eggs	marmalade
2½ oz. sponge cake	2 oz. sugar for pudding
or breadcrumbs	with cake crumbs or
¾ pint milk	3 oz. sugar with
2 oz. sugar for the	breadcrumbs (this makes
meringue	a sweet pudding so can
	be reduced if wished)

1 Spread the marmalade at the bottom of a pie dish.

2 Separate eggs.

3 Heat the milk and pour over the crumbs, allow to cool slightly, then whisk in the egg yolks and sugar.

4 Whisk together well and pour into the dish.

5 Stand in another dish of cold water and bake for approximately 45 minutes in the centre of a very moderate oven (350°F.—Gas Mark 3) until the pudding feels quite firm.

6 Drain the mandarin oranges and arrange most of them on top of the pudding.

7 Whisk egg whites and fold in the sugar.

8 Pile on top of the sweet and return to the oven for a further 20 minutes.

9 Decorate with remaining mandarin oranges.

Queen of puddings

An ordinary queen of puddings is made exactly like the orange one (see preceding recipe) but flavour the crumb and custard mixture with a little grated lemon rind and spread the pudding with jam.

Pancakes

cooking time   2 minutes each pancake

you will need:

4 oz. plain flour	pinch salt
1 egg	½ pint milk
fat or oil	

1 Sift the flour and salt into a bowl.

2 Make a well in the centre of the flour.

3 Break into it the egg.

4 Gradually add the milk and stir with a wooden spoon until the batter is smooth.

5 Leave the batter to stand at least 30 minutes.

6 Heat a frying-pan with fat or oil

7 When hot, drain off as much fat as possible.

8 Take a measure, such as a tablespoon, depending on the size of the pan, and pour in enough batter to coat the pan very thinly and evenly or put batter into jug for easy pouring.

9 Cook over a fairly fierce heat until 1 side is cooked.

10 Toss the pancake or turn over using a palette knife.

11 Cook the other side.

12 Pancakes can be reheated in the oven if they are well covered with buttered greaseproof paper.

Pineapple surprise pudding

cooking time   40 minutes

you will need:

½ pint pineapple juice (bottled or canned)	2 oz. butter
2 oz. flour (plain or self-raising)	2 oz. castor sugar
	2 large eggs
little canned pineapple	few drops pineapple essence (if wished)

1 Cream together the butter and sugar.

2 Separate eggs.

3 Add the egg yolks and flour to butter mixture then the pineapple juice and pineapple essence.

4 The mixture is very soft and will probably curdle but this does not matter.

5 Lastly fold in the very stiffly beaten egg whites.

6 Pour into a buttered dish, stand this in another dish of cold water.

7 Bake for approximately 40 minutes in the centre of a very moderate oven (350°F.—Gas Mark 3).

8 Decorate with pineapple.

9 This sweet separates during cooking giving a soufflé-like top and pineapple sauce.

Chunky apricot pudding

cooking time   1½ hours

you will need:

8 oz. self-raising flour	4 oz. good quality dried apricots, cut into pieces
4 oz. butter or margarine	¼ level teaspoon salt
1 egg	¼ pint milk
3 oz. castor sugar	2 tablespoons orange marmalade

1 Sift together flour and salt.

2 Rub in fat, add sugar.

3 Mix to a soft batter with the egg and milk.

4 Stir in apricots.

5 Spoon marmalade into a well greased, 2-pint sized pudding basin, two-thirds fill with the apricot mixture, then cover with greased paper or foil.

6 Steam steadily for 1½ hours or steam in 6 individual pudding basins for about 25 minutes. *Note:* If the apricots are very hard and dry soak in water for an hour or two, drain well and shake in a kitchen cloth or absorbent paper before chopping.

Rhubarb and date plate pie

cooking time   40 minutes

you will need:

8 oz. short crust pastry (see page 63)	4 oz. chopped dates
	1 lb. rhubarb
little water or use grated rind and juice of 1 lemon instead	2–3 oz. sugar
	flour or semolina
	whole dates (to decorate)

1 Line a pie plate or sandwich tin with half the pastry, sprinkling with little flour or semolina to prevent fruit softening bottom of pastry.

2 Put the chopped rhubarb, dates and sugar over this, together with 1 tablespoon water or lemon juice – no more – over the fruit.

3 Cover with the rest of the pastry, seal the edges and give the pie a fluted edge.

4 Brush pastry with a little water and sugar to give a glaze.

5 Bake in centre of moderately hot oven (425°F.—Gas Mark 6) for 20 minutes then lower heat for further 20 minutes.

6 Decorate with whole dates in centre.

Rice meringue

cooking time   35 minutes

you will need:

2 cups cooked milk pudding	2 eggs
either 1 cup more milk or 1 cup apple purée	3 tablespoons sugar few cherries to decorate

1 Add milk or fruit purée and the beaten egg yolks to pudding.
2 Taste, and stir in a little sugar if wished.
3 Pour into a pie dish and heat for 20 minutes in moderate oven (375°F.—Gas Mark 4).
4 Whisk egg whites until stiff, fold in sugar and pile on the pudding.
5 Top with cherries and brown in oven for about 15 minutes.

Rice cream. Beat a little cream or evaporated milk into left-over rice pudding. Add a small quantity of fruit juice to flavour. Put into sundae glasses and top with fruit and cream.

Rice puddings

cooking time   2–3 hours

you will need:

2–3 oz. of round rice	1 oz. sugar
1 pint milk	

1 Wash the rice.
2 Put it into a dish with the sugar and milk and cook in slow oven (275–300°F.—Gas Mark 1–2) for 2–3 hours until creamy.

Variations on this

1 If you are in a hurry just cover the rice with a little cold water. Start it in a really hot oven for 10 minutes then pour the hot milk, add the sugar, stir briskly, lower the heat and cook for about 1 hour.
2 Add a good knob of butter or little suet for extra creaminess. You must stir after about 30 minutes cooking, to mix butter in well.
3 Use evaporated milk instead of some of the fresh milk.

Boiled rice pudding

Instead of cooking in the oven, cook the rice in a double saucepan over hot water. This will take approximately 45 minutes–1 hour.

Spiced plum cobbler

cooking time   45–50 minutes

you will need:

1½ lb. plums	8 oz. flour (with plain
½ level teaspoon mixed spice	flour 2 level teaspoons baking powder)
4 oz. luxury margarine	2 oz. castor sugar
2 tablespoons milk	1 egg
3–4 oz. demerara sugar	milk and sugar to coat

1 Wash the plums, halve them and remove the stones.
2 Place in a 2 pint oven-ware dish with the demerara sugar and spice.

3 Bake in the centre of a moderately hot oven (400°F.—Gas Mark 5) for 15 minutes.
4 Sieve the flour into a bowl.
5 Add the luxury margarine and rub in until the mixture resembles fine breadcrumbs.
6 Add the sugar, egg and milk to mix to a soft but not sticky dough.
7 Turn on to a lightly floured board and knead lightly with the fingertips. Roll out to a ½ inch in thickness.
8 Cut into rounds with a 2 inch fluted cutter and with ½-inch fluted cutter, remove the centres.
9 Place slightly overlapping on top of the half-cooked plums.
10 Brush with milk and sprinkle with sugar.
11 Return to the centre of a moderately hot oven (400°F.—Gas Mark 5) for 30–35 minutes.
12 Apples, damsons, mixed fruit are all excellent cooked this way.

Sponge pudding

cooking time   1½ hours

you will need:

4 oz. margarine or butter	2 large eggs little milk
4 oz. sugar	6 oz. flour (with plain
flavouring (I give lots of these below)	flour use 1½ level teaspoons baking powder)

1 Cream margarine and sugar.
2 Gradually beat in the eggs.
3 Stir in the flour and enough milk to give a soft mixture, so that it drops easily from the spoon.
4 Add flavourings then put into well greased basin. Don't fill the basin too high.
5 Cover with greased paper and a cloth or a second layer of paper.
6 Steam for a good 1½ hours over rapidly boiling water.

Flavourings

Jam sponge
Put several good spoonfuls of jam at the bottom and serve with jam sauce (see page 64).
Lemon or orange sponge
Add grated rind of 1 lemon or orange to the mixture and mix with the fruit as well as milk. Put marmalade at the bottom if wished and serve with a lemon or orange sauce (see page 64).
Ginger sponge
Sieve 1 or 2 teaspoons powdered ginger with the flour. Put a good layer of golden syrup at the bottom of the basin and then serve it with a syrup sauce (see page 64).

Prune sponge

Put a good layer of cooked stoned prunes at the bottom of the basin. Use the juice as sauce.

Chocolate sponge

Instead of 6 oz. flour use 5 oz. flour and 1 oz. cocoa, add a dessertspoon of golden syrup to the margarine and sugar. Serve with a really good egg custard or chocolate sauce.

Fruit sponge

Add about 4–6 oz. fruit. Mixed fruit, chopped cherries or raisins can be used.

10 do's and don'ts for making pastry

1 Do weigh and measure most carefully for good pastry depends on the right proportion of fat to flour.
2 Do try to keep your hands and utensils cool. In hot weather run cold water over your wrists.
3 Do use a large bowl when rubbing fat into flour for pastry, and lift the mixture in the air as high as you can. This keeps the mixture light and introduces as much air as possible.
4 Do rub the fat into the flour with your forefinger and thumb. If you rub with the palm of your hand you exclude air and make a tougher pastry.
5 Don't over-handle the dough. Roll briskly and firmly in one direction. Don't roll in all directions.
6 Don't over-flour the pastry board or rolling-pin. This spoils the original proportion of fat to flour.
7 Don't make the pastry dough too wet. This means over-cooking and a tough pastry.
8 Don't make the pastry dough too dry. This means you have to knead very hard to try and bind it together which gives a very short and over-crumbly pastry that is difficult to shape and cut.
9 Do edge pastry attractively:
   (a) Make a narrow plait, using thin strips of pastry and edge your pie or flan with this.
   (b) Flute the pastry with a knife using your thumbs as a guide to the rounds. Rough up the edges of pastry as you go with the blade of the knife.
10 Do bake pastry quickly. With plate tarts, etc., it is a good idea to set the pastry in a hot oven, then, when becoming brown, to lower the heat to make sure filling, etc., is cooked.

American biscuit crust

cooking time   12–15 minutes

you will need:

8 oz. flour	1 dessertspoon sugar
4 level teaspoons baking powder (or 2 level teaspoons with self-raising flour)	(if using pastry for sweet dish)
	water or milk to mix
good pinch salt	1–2 oz. fat preferably vegetable shortening

1 This recipe is very economical in its use of fat. If it is eaten the day it is baked, and preferably hot, it is very good.
2 Sieve flour, baking powder and salt together.
3 Rub in fat. Add sugar, if used.
4 Mix to rolling consistency with cold water.
5 Roll out rather thinly as this pastry will rise a great deal.
6 Never keep this pastry standing before it is baked.
7 Bake in a very hot oven (450–475°F.—Gas Mark 7–8) for 12–15 minutes.

Choux pastry

cooking time   35 minutes

you will need:

3 oz. flour (plain or self-raising)	1 oz. margarine or butter
1 gill water	2 whole eggs and yolk of 1 egg (or 3 small eggs)
pinch sugar	

1 Put water, margarine (or butter) and sugar into a saucepan.
2 Heat gently till fat has melted.
3 Remove from heat.
4 Stir in flour.
5 Return pan to low heat and cook very gently but thoroughly, stirring all the time until mixture is dry enough to form a ball and leave pan clean.
6 Once again remove pan from heat and gradually add well beaten eggs.
7 Do this slowly to produce a perfectly smooth mixture.
8 Allow to cool then use for cream buns and éclairs.

Cream buns

cooking time   35–40 minutes

you will need:

choux pastry (see preceding recipe) cream	icing sugar or flavoured water icing to cover

1 The most simple method is to grease and flour individual patty tins and put in a spoonful of the mixture or pile some of the mixture on to well greased and floured baking trays.
2 The correct method, however, is to put the mixture into piping bags and force through large plain pipes on to the floured and greased baking trays.
3 If you have a deep tin which can be put right over the cakes while in the oven, use this, for it helps to give a far better shape to them.

4 The tin should be light in weight and allow several inches in height, for buns will rise considerably as they cook.
5 It is still quite possible to bake the buns without the tin.
6 Put the tray of cakes into the centre of a hot oven (450°F.—Gas Mark 7) for 35 minutes (allow a good 5 minutes extra cooking time if they are covered).
7 For the last 20 minutes reduce the heat (400°F.—Gas Mark 5).
8 At the end of this time the buns should be pale golden in colour, and feel very firm and crisp.
9 Cool them gradually and away from a draught.
10 You may sometimes find that when you split the buns there is a little uncooked pastry left in the centre. This should be taken out carefully, and if you feel it necessary the buns returned for a few minutes to a cool oven to dry.
11 When you are quite sure the buns are cold split them and fill with cream.
12 Cover with sieved icing sugar or chocolate or coffee flavoured water icing (see page 82).

Flaky pastry (for sausage rolls, mince pies etc.)

you will need:

8 oz. plain flour	pinch salt
5–6 oz. fat*	water to mix

*Use any of the following:

All butter.
All table margarine or superfine or luxury margarine.
⅔ table margarine and ⅓ modern whipped-up light fat or pure cooking fat.

1 Sieve flour with salt.
2 Divide fat into 3 portions.
3 Rub 1 portion into flour in usual way.
4 Mix to rolling consistency with cold water.
5 Roll out to oblong shape. Now take the second portion of fat, divide it into small pieces and lay them on surface of ⅔ of dough.
6 Leave remaining ⅓ without fat.
7 Take its 2 corners and fold back over second ⅓ so that the dough looks like an envelope with its flap open.
8 Fold over top end of pastry, so closing the 'envelope'.
9 Turn pastry at right angles, seal open ends of pastry and 'rib' it.
10 This means depressing it with the rolling-pin at intervals, so giving a corrugated effect and equalising the pressure of air. This makes it certain that the pastry will rise evenly.

11 Repeat the process again using the remaining fat and turning pastry in same way.
12 Roll out pastry once more, but should it begin to feel very soft and sticky put it into a cold place for 30 minutes to become firm before rolling out.
13 Fold pastry as before, turn it, seal edges and 'rib' it.
14 Altogether the pastry should have 3 foldings and 3 rollings. It is then ready to stand in a cold place for a little while before baking, since the contrast between the cold and the heat of the oven makes the pastry rise better.
15 To bake, use a very hot oven (475°F.—Gas Mark 8) for the first 15 minutes, after this lower the Gas Mark to 5 or 6, or turn the electric oven off to finish cooking for remaining time at a lower temperature.

Flan pastry or biscuit crust (for sweet flans and fruit tarts)

cooking time   according to individual recipe

you will need:

8 oz. flour	cold water or yolk 1 egg
4 oz. fat*	to bind
pinch salt	2 dessertspoons sugar

*Margarine or butter is excellent for this pastry.

1 Cream fat and sugar together until light in colour.
2 Sieve flour and salt together and add to creamed fat, mixing with a knife.
3 Gradually add enough water, or egg and water, to make a firm rolling consistency.
4 Use fingertips to feel the pastry (see page 64).
5 Bake in a hot oven (425–450°F.—Gas Mark 6–7).
6 To line flan put pastry over case and press down base and sides firmly then roll over top with rolling pin for a good edge. Decorate edge as wished.

Short crust pastry (for all general purposes)

you will need:

8 oz. flour	approx. 2 tablespoons
4 oz. fat*	cold water to mix
good pinch salt	

*There are many fats and combinations of fat that give a first class short crust pastry. Choose between:
Modern whipped light fat. Use 3½ oz. only as it is very rich.
Pure cooking fat or lard.
Margarine—for best results use a table margarine, a superfine or luxury margarine.
Butter or
perhaps the favourite of all—2 oz. margarine and 2 oz. cooking fat.

1 Sieve flour and salt and rub in fat until mixture looks like fine breadcrumbs.
2 Using first a knife and then the fingertips to feel the pastry, gradually add enough cold water to make the dough into a rolling consistency.
3 Lightly flour the rolling-pin and pastry board.
4 If a great deal of flour is necessary to roll out the pastry then you have undoubtedly made it too wet.
5 Roll pastry to required thickness and shape, lifting and turning it to keep it light.
6 Exact cooking times for pastry are given in the recipes but as a general rule it should be cooked in a hot oven (425–450°F.—Gas Mark 6–7).

Suet crust (for savoury or sweet puddings)

cooking time   according to individual recipe

you will need:

8 oz. flour (self-raising flour, or plain flour with 2 level teaspoons baking powder)	pinch salt water to mix 2–4 oz. finely shredded suet

1 Sieve flour, salt and baking powder.
2 Add suet. Mix to a rolling consistency with cold water.
3 Roll out thinly as this pastry rises.

Puff pastry (for vol-au-vent cases, vanilla slices, cream horns etc.)

you will need:

8 oz. plain flour 7–8 oz. fat* cold water to mix	good pinch salt few drops lemon juice

*You have a good choice of fat here. Use:
Butter.
Table or luxury margarine.
⅔ margarine and ⅓ modern whipped-up light fat, or lard.

1 Sieve flour and salt together.
2 Mix to rolling consistency with cold water and lemon juice.
3 Roll to oblong shape.
4 Make fat into neat block and place in centre of pastry and fold over it first the bottom section of pastry, and then the top section so that the fat is quite covered.
5 Turn the dough at right angles, seal edges and 'rib' carefully (see flaky pastry, page 63) and roll out.
6 Fold dough into envelope, turn it, seal edges, 'rib' and roll again.
7 Repeat 5 times, so making 7 rollings and 7 foldings in all.
8 It will be necessary to put pastry to rest in cold place once or twice between rollings to prevent it becoming sticky and soft.

9 Always put it to rest before rolling it for the last time, and before baking.
10 Bake in very hot oven (to make it rise, and keep in the fat). Bake for the first 10–15 minutes at 475–500°F.—Gas Mark 8–9, then lower to Gas Mark 5–6 or turn electric oven right out and re-set to 400°F. to finish cooking at lower temperature.
11 Well made puff pastry should rise to 4 or 5 times its original thickness.
12 When making vol-au-vent cases it may be necessary to remove a little soft dough and return to oven to dry out.

Custard sauce

cooking time   10–15 minutes

1 Make with custard powder, following the directions given by the manufacturers.
2 OR use a fresh egg, beaten with 1 tablespoon of sugar and ½ pint of warm milk.
3 Cook in a jug standing in a pan of hot water or the top of a double saucepan until the custard is thick enough to coat the back of a wooden spoon.

Jam sauce or syrup sauce

cooking time   4–5 minutes

you will need:

4 good tablespoons jam	juice of 1 lemon 2–3 tablespoons water

Boil together until jam has melted or use golden syrup instead.

Orange sauce

cooking time   10 minutes

you will need:

2–3 oranges 4 oz. sugar	½ pint water

1 Simmer few thin strips of orange rind in little water until soft. Drain.
2 Make syrup of the sugar and water. Simmer rind in this for about 10 minutes.
3 Add pieces of orange.

Lemon sauce

As in preceding recipe.
1 But if using 3 lemons you may find you need a little extra sugar, and instead of putting in pieces of lemon add the lemon juice.
2 If a thicker sauce is required either in this or the orange sauce, blend 1 good teaspoon of lemon or arrowroot with the mixture and boil until thick.

Sweet white sauce

cooking time   5–8 minutes

you will need:

1 tablespoon cornflour	1 oz. sugar
½ pint milk	little vanilla essence
½ oz. butter	

1 Blend the cornflour with a little cold milk.
2 Bring the rest of the milk to the boil.
3 Pour over the cornflour and return to the pan with the sugar.

4 Continue to cook steadily until smooth and thick.
5 Add the essence.
6 Serve with steamed puddings.

Chapter 10

Tea Time—Bread and Scones

There are few things that cause more satisfaction than a perfectly baked loaf of home-made bread or scones hot from the oven. And even in these days when most people are very pressed for time it is worth spending a short while making something special for the family to enjoy.

Bread making

The following is a basic recipe to use. Flours vary slightly in the amount of liquid they absorb so do not be worried if you need a little more than this recipe.

The amount of salt varies a great deal according to personal taste. The first time use the smaller quantity. Don't be alarmed by the terms used in bread recipes. 'Proving' simply means to let the dough rise, and you must not try to hurry this too much otherwise you will kill the yeast which, unlike baking powder and other raising agents, is a living thing.

White bread

cooking time   40–55 minutes

you will need:

3 lb. plain white flour	1–2 level teaspoons
1¼ pints tepid water	sugar
(at least)	1 oz. fresh yeast*
	or ½ oz. dried yeast
	3–5 level teaspoons salt

*With dried yeast mix with the sugar and a little tepid liquid. Allow to stand in warm place until soft—approximately 20 minutes, then cream. Continue after this as for fresh yeast.

1 Sieve flour and salt into warm basin, then put into warm place.
2 Cream yeast and sugar in another basin.
3 Add part of liquid.
4 Put this into a well, made in the centre of the flour, giving a light dusting of flour over the top.
5 Cover with a clean cloth, leave in a warm place for a good 15 minutes until top is covered with bubbles.

6 Add rest of liquid (you may need a little more than this) but have a soft dough.
7 Knead well until dough is smooth and leaves bowl clean.
8 To test if adequately kneaded press with finger, if impression comes out the dough is sufficiently kneaded.
9 Put to rise in warm place for about 1½ hours, then knead again.
10 Form into loaves, and put into warmed and lightly greased bread tins, half filling them.
11 If you wish to give a very crisp crust, brush with a little melted margarine or use milk or egg and water.
12 Prove for final time—about 20 minutes.
13 Bake in the centre of a hot oven (425–450°F. —Gas Mark 6–7) for the first 10 minutes.
14 Reduce heat to 375°F.—Gas Mark 4, for a further 30–45 minutes, depending on the size of the loaves.
15 TO TEST. Knock on bottom of loaves and they should sound hollow.
16 Cool away from draught.
Note: An ounce of lard or margarine rubbed into flour helps to keep the bread moist.

Shaping bread

Bloomer loaf: Form the dough into a rather 'fat' roll. Flatten the top slightly, then mark on top with a sharp knife before final proving. Bake on flat baking tins.

Cottage loaf: Form the dough into two rounds, one considerably smaller than the other. Press the small round on top of the larger and make a deep thumb mark in the middle of the top round. Bake on flat baking tins.

French stick: Use basic bread dough or richer dough in Vienna breakfast rolls. Form into long 'stick' shape. Score on top with a sharp knife before proving.

Coburg: Form dough into large rounds. Mark with wide cross on top before proving. Bake on flat baking tins.

French or Vienna loaf: Form into a rather shorter and thicker 'stick' than the French stick.

Farmhouse or Danish loaf: If using the basic bread dough, mix with rather more milk than water. This can be baked in a loaf tin, but fill the tin slightly fuller than usual, so you get the typical rounded edges. Score well on top before final proving. Brush with a little milk and sprinkle on top with light dusting of flour before baking.

Brown bread

Follow the same method as in preceding recipe, but use half wholemeal flour. You do need to make a slightly stickier dough for good results.

Wholemeal bread

Use the same method as for white bread but add sufficient liquid to give a really sticky dough. This means instead of kneading with your fingers you have to beat with a wooden spoon. It will also mean a little extra baking.

Fruit bread (no yeast)

cooking time   35 minutes

you will need:

8 oz. flour (with plain flour use 2 level teaspoons baking powder)	4 oz. dried fruit (or more if wished)
	1 oz. mixed peel
	2 oz. margarine
1 teaspoon grated lemon rind	1 or 2 eggs
2–3 oz. sugar	milk to mix

1 Sieve flour and baking powder.
2 Rub in margarine, add sugar and rest of ingredients, stirring in enough milk to give sticky consistency.
3 Put into well greased and floured loaf tin.
4 Bake for 35 minutes in the centre of a moderate oven (375°F.—Gas Mark 4).

Croissants

cooking time   20 minutes

you will need:

1 lb. plain flour*	1 oz. fresh yeast or 1 level tablespoon dried yeast
1 oz. lard	
2 level (medium) teaspoons salt	

egg wash:

1 egg, beaten	1 egg
4 oz. margarine*	little water
	½ teaspoon sugar

*Use strong flour and a tough waxy margarine if possible.

1 If using fresh yeast blend into ½ pint water less 2 tablespoons. If using dried yeast sprinkle on ½ pint less 2 tablespoons warm water with 1 teaspoon sugar. Allow to stand until frothy, about 10 minutes.
2 Mix dry ingredients and rub in lard.
3 Add yeast liquid and egg and mix to a dough.
4 Knead on a lightly floured board until dough is smooth.
5 Roll the dough into a long strip approximately $20 \times 6 \times \frac{1}{4}$ inches thick, taking care to keep the dough piece rectangular.
6 Divide the margarine into 3 equal parts. Use 1 part to dot the dough, covering the top two-thirds of the surface and leaving a small border clear.
7 Fold in 3 by bringing up the undotted flap of the dough, then bringing the top part over.
8 Turn the dough half a turn so that the open ends are parallel to the rolling pin. Seal the edges by pressing with the rolling pin.
9 Re-shape to a long strip by gently pressing the dough at intervals with the rolling pin. Again take care to keep the dough pieces rectangular.
10 Repeat with the other two-thirds of the margarine.
11 Place in a greased polythene bag and allow to 'prove', i.e. rise in the refrigerator for 30 minutes. Roll out as before to a rectangular strip.
12 Repeat folding and rolling 3 times more.
13 Place in the refrigerator for at least 1 hour. The dough can be stored overnight at this stage.

To shape the croissants

14 Roll out to ½ inch thick on the table, cover with greased polythene or paper and leave for 30 minutes.
15 Roll out to a rectangle slightly bigger than 12 × 18 inches and trim to this size. Divide in half lengthwise. Each strip should make 5 triangles with a 6-inch base and 6 inches high.
16 Brush with egg wash, made by mixing egg, water and sugar.
17 Roll up towards point, curving into crescent shapes as you roll and finish with the tip underneath.
18 After shaping, put them on ungreased baking

sheet, cover with greased polythene and leave about 30 minutes until light and spongy.

19 Before baking brush lightly with egg wash. Bake on middle shelf of·hot oven (450°F.—Gas Mark 7) for 20 minutes.

Note: When making croissants keep dough and margarine equally *cool* and work *quickly.* Keep edges of dough straight and corners square.

Suggestions for any left-over dough

Palmiers
1 Pile pastry ends together.
2 Roll out to rectangle.
3 Sprinkle with sugar and cinnamon.
4 Fold in 3 and roll as for croissants.
5 Again dredge with sugar and spice.
6 Roll up firmly like a Swiss roll.
7 Cut pinwheel slices.
8 Put on greased baking sheet.
9 Allow to 'prove' in warm place until puffy.
10 Bake 10 minutes in hot oven.

Rolls
1 Knead trimmings to a smooth dough.
2 Shape in round rolls.
3 'Prove' and bake as above.

Vienna or rich yeast rolls

cooking time   15–20 minutes

you will need:

1 lb. plain flour	½ oz. yeast
1 teaspoon salt	2 oz. butter or margarine
½ pint tepid milk	1 beaten egg
1 teaspoon sugar	

1 Sieve together the flour and salt.
2 Warm slightly, then rub in margarine.
3 Make a well in centre of mixture, cream yeast and sugar.
4 Add milk and nearly all beaten egg and pour into well.
5 Form into an elastic dough and beat thoroughly by hand.
6 Leave to rise, covered, in a warm place until the dough has doubled in bulk.
7 Turn on to floured board.
8 Knead well and divide into 12 pieces.
9 Shape into plaits, round rolls, crescents and miniature loaves and place on to well-greased baking trays.
10 Leave to rise again for 15–20 minutes.
11 Brush with beaten egg.
12 Bake in hot oven (450°F.—Gas Mark 7) for 15–20 minutes.

Date bread

cooking time   55 minutes

you will need:

1 oz. butter	1 or 2 oz. sugar
8 oz. self-raising flour	12 oz. dates
1 gill water	1 egg

1 Heat butter and water, pour over chopped dates.
2 Allow to cool, then stir in flour, sugar and beaten egg.
3 Mix thoroughly, put into greased loaf tin and bake for approximately 55 minutes in centre of a moderate oven (375°F.—Gas Mark 4).

Soda bread

cooking time   25 minutes

you will need:

8 oz. plain flour	1 gill milk
1 level teaspoon bicarbonate of soda	approximately 1 oz. margarine
1 level teaspoon cream of tartar	pinch salt

1 Rub the margarine into the flour, this is not essential, but helps to keep the bread moist.
2 Add the salt.
3 Dissolve the bicarbonate of soda and cream of tartar in the milk.
4 Add to the flour.
5 Knead lightly and form into a round loaf.
6 Brush with a little milk and bake on a flat tin in the centre of a very hot oven (475°F.—Gas Mark 8) for 15 minutes.
7 After this time, lower the gas to moderately hot (Gas Mark 5), or reset electric cooker to 400°F. for another 10–15 minutes.
8 If using sour milk omit cream of tartar.

Drop scones or Scotch pancakes

cooking time   2–3 minutes

you will need:

4 oz. flour (with plain flour use either 2 teaspoons baking powder or ½ small teaspoon bicarbonate of soda and 1 small teaspoon cream of tartar)	pinch salt
	1 oz. sugar
	1 egg
	1 gill milk
	1 oz. melted margarine (not essential)

1 Sieve together dry ingredients.
2 Beat in first egg, then milk.
3 Lastly stir in melted margarine.
4 This is not essential but it does help to keep the scones moist.
5 Grease and warm the girdle, electric hot-plate or frying pan.
6 It is best to use the bottom of the frying pan—the part that usually goes over the heat, if very clean.
7 To test if correct heat, drop a teaspoon of the mixture on this and if it goes golden brown within 1 minute the plate is ready.
8 Drop spoonfuls of the batter on to the plate.

9 Cook for about 2 minutes, then turn and cook for a further 2 minutes.

10 To test whether cooked press firmly with the back of a knife and if no batter comes from the sides and the scones feel firm, cool in a wire sieve.

Plain scones

cooking time   approximately 10 minutes

you will need:

8 oz. flour (with plain flour use either 4 level teaspoons baking powder OR 1 level teaspoon cream of tartar and ½ teaspoon bicarbonate of soda.	With self raising flour you CAN use half above if desired) 1 oz. sugar 1–2 oz. margarine good pinch salt milk to mix*

*If using sour milk, which is excellent for mixing scones, then you can omit the cream of tartar. Or if using baking powder use half quantity only.

1 Sieve together flour, salt, bicarbonate of soda and cream of tartar.

2 Rub in the margarine, add the sugar.

3 Mix to a *soft* rolling consistency with the milk.

4 Roll out and cut into required shapes.

5 Put on to an ungreased tin (unless cheese, oatmeal or treacle in the ingredients).

6 Bake near the top of a very hot oven (475°F. —Gas Mark 8) for approximately 10 minutes.

7 To test if cooked press firmly at the sides.

8 Scones are cooked when they feel firm to the touch.

Brown scones

Use above recipe, but 4 oz. wholemeal (stone ground) flour and 4 oz. white flour.

Fruit scones

Use above recipe but add 2–4 oz. chopped dried fruit, sultanas, raisins, currants, dates, glacé cherries or a mixture.

Almond scones

Use above recipe but add 1 oz. sugar extra and 2–3 oz. blanched chopped almonds. Stir a few drops almond essence into milk for mixing. Sprinkle chopped almonds on top before baking.

Marmalade scones

Use above recipe but substitute 2 tablespoons marmalade for the sugar.

Treacle scones

Use above recipe but add 1 tablespoon treacle and sieve pinch cinnamon with flour. Omit sugar.

Oatmeal scones

Use half flour, half fine oatmeal in above recipe.

Cheese scones

Sieve plenty of seasoning with flour. Add 2–3 oz. grated cheese and omit sugar.

Cheese and ham scone whirls

cooking time   10–15 minutes

you will need:

8 oz. self-raising flour	1 level teaspoon salt
2 oz. butter or margarine	1 egg approx. 5 tablespoons milk
3 oz. Cheddar cheese	
2 oz. lean ham	

1 Grate cheese and chop the ham.

2 Sift together flour and salt.

3 Rub in fat then mix to a soft, but not sticky dough with egg and milk.

4 Turn out on to a floured board. Knead lightly till smooth then roll into an oblong approximately 6 × 8 inches.

5 Brush all over with milk then sprinkle with cheese and ham to within ½ inch of edges.

6 Roll up like a Swiss roll starting from one of the longer sides, then cut into ½ inch slices.

7 Put on to greased baking trays and bake in the centre of a hot oven (425–450°F.—Gas Mark 7) for 10–15 minutes.

Potato scones

cooking time   10–12 minutes

you will need:

8 oz. freshly boiled mashed potatoes	flour use 2 level teaspoons baking powder; with self-raising flour use 1 level teaspoon baking powder)
1 egg	
2 oz. melted butter or margarine	
4 oz. flour (with plain	salt

1 Mash or sieve potatoes while still hot.

2 Add flour, salt and melted butter.

3 Mix well, add enough beaten egg to make a stiff mixture.

4 Roll out to ¾ inch thickness and cut into rounds or triangles.

5 Put on baking sheet and bake near top of hot oven (450°F.—Gas Mark 7) for approximately 10–12 minutes, until golden brown.

6 Split and serve hot with plenty of butter.

Chapter 11
Tea Time—Small Cakes and Pastries

An appetizing batch of small cakes or tarts is bound to be a success at the family tea table. And in general, they are usually quicker and easier to make than a large cake, which is a great boon to the busy housewife.

Banana chiffon tartlets

cooking time   10–15 minutes

you will need:

6–8 oz. pastry (flaky or short crust, see page 63)	3 large bananas
	1 lemon jelly
little whipped cream	2 eggs
2 oz. sugar	¾ pint water

1 Line the patty tins with pastry and bake 'blind'.
2 Dissolve the jelly in water, pour on to the well-beaten egg yolks and sugar.
3 When cool, but not set, add 2 mashed bananas and the stiffly beaten egg whites.
4 Pile into the cooked and cooled pastry cases.
5 When quite set decorate with cream and the sliced banana.

Butterscotch fingers

cooking time   8–10 minutes

you will need:

8 thin slices of bread	apricot jam
2 oz. margarine	2 oz. brown sugar
2 oz. golden syrup	few nuts to decorate

1 Remove crust and sandwich slices of bread with apricot jam.
2 Cut each sandwich into fingers.
3 Melt margarine, sugar and syrup in frying pan until the sugar has melted.
4 Cook fingers in this mixture, turning over until golden brown on both sides.
5 Serve at once topped with chopped nuts.
6 This is equally successful as a hot sweet or quick simple cake for tea.

Chocolate boats

cooking time   25 minutes

you will need:

4 oz. puff pastry (see page 64)	2 oz. margarine
	2 oz. sugar
2 eggs	2 oz. chocolate powder
3 oz. fine cake or chocolate biscuit crumbs	chocolate or coffee glacé icing (see page 82)
apricot jam	1 tablespoon flour
vanilla essence	

1 Roll out the pastry very thinly and line boat-shaped tins with it.
2 Cream together the margarine and sugar, add the beaten egg yolks, vanilla essence, crumbs and flour.
3 Mix thoroughly, then add the chocolate powder.
4 Lastly fold in the stiffly beaten egg whites.
5 Put spoonfuls of this mixture into the tarts.
6 Bake in the centre of a hot oven (450°F.—Gas Mark 7) for 25 minutes.
7 Reduce the heat to moderate after the first 15 minutes.
8 When cold cover with coffee or chocolate glacé icing.

Coconut pyramids

cooking time   15–20 minutes

you will need:

2 stiffly beaten egg whites	cherries, angelica (if wished)
6 oz. desiccated coconut	3 oz. castor sugar
	1 dessertspoon cornflour

1 Mix coconut, cornflour and sugar together.
2 Work into the egg whites until a firm mixture.
3 If egg whites are very large do not use all of them.
4 Form into pyramids with your fingers and either put on to a well greased baking tin or rice paper on a tin.
5 Bake in centre of a very moderate oven, (350°F.—Gas Mark 3), until pale golden brown on top. Handle carefully until cold.
6 Decorate with cherries and angelica if wished.

Chocolate coconut pyramids
Omit cornflour and add 1 rounded dessertspoon cocoa. When set pour a little melted chocolate on to pyramids. Decorate with cherries.

Cornish lady fingers

cooking time   15–20 minutes

you will need:

1 lb. flour	3 tablespoons sugar
4–8 oz. dried fruit	water
8 oz. lard	

1 Rub half the lard into flour and mix with sugar and water as for pastry.
2 Roll out thinly, spread with half remaining lard and fruit, fold in 3 and re-roll.

3 Do the same with the rest of lard and fruit.

4 Give one final rolling, cut into fingers, brush top with milk and bake in hot oven for 15–20 minutes, (425–450°F.—Gas Mark 6–7).

Cream horns

cooking time   15 minutes

you will need:

8 oz. puff pastry (see page 64)	icing sugar
	whipped or mock cream
little castor sugar	jam
egg white	milk

1 Roll out the pastry until about the thickness of a penny.

2 Cut it into long strips 1 inch wide.

3 If you can cut these 'on the cross' you will get a better shaped cornet.

4 Roll carefully round the horn cases (these metal cases can be bought) brush lightly with milk on the joints.

5 Be careful not to stretch the pastry.

6 Brush with either a little more milk and dust with castor sugar or use egg white and sugar.

7 Bake for 10–15 minutes near the top of a very hot oven (475°F.—Gas Mark 8).

8 Cool slightly, then gently withdraw the cases.

9 When the pastry is quite cold fill with jam and cream. Dust with icing sugar.

Custard tarts

cooking time   40 minutes

you will need:

6 oz. short crust pastry (see page 63)	2 eggs
	½ pint milk
3 dessertspoons sugar	nutmeg
½ oz. butter	vanilla essence

1 Line patty tins with the pastry and bake 'blind' for 7–10 minutes in hot oven.

2 Beat the eggs and the sugar.

3 Warm the milk slightly, mix with the eggs, add butter, vanilla essence and nutmeg.

4 Pour into pastry cases and cook in coolest part of moderate oven (375°F.—Gas Mark 4) until set, approximately 25–30 minutes.

Eccles cakes

cooking time   20 minutes

you will need:

8 oz. puff pastry (see page 64)	2 oz. sugar
	grated rind and juice of 1 lemon
2 oz. sultanas	
2 oz. candied peel	extra sugar and water or egg white (to glaze)
good pinch mixed spice	
2 oz. currants	
2 oz. margarine	

1 Roll pastry into large rounds about the size of a saucer.

2 Mix remaining ingredients. See Banbury cakes for method of blending.

3 Put spoonfuls of mixture in the centre of each round then pick up all the edges.

4 Seal with water, then turn rounds upside down and flatten with rolling pin.

5 Mark 2 or 3 cuts on the top, brush with water and sugar or egg white and sugar, bake in the centre of a hot oven (450°F.—Gas Mark 7) for about 20 minutes.

6 Reduce heat after 15 minutes if the cakes are becoming too brown.

Banbury cakes

cooking time   20 minutes

you will need:

As for Eccles cakes but add 2 oz. cake crumbs or crumbled macaroon biscuits. Milk and castor sugar to glaze.

1 Roll out the pastry until it is the thickness of a penny.

2 Cut into large oval shapes.

3 Cream the margarine and sugar together then work in all the ingredients.

4 Put a spoonful of this mixture on one half the pastry.

5 Fold over then press edges very firmly together.

6 If necessary brush with a little milk or water to seal them.

7 Shape with a rolling pin and your fingers until you have ovals.

8 Make 2 or 3 splits on the top.

9 Brush lightly with milk and castor sugar.

10 Bake in the centre of a hot oven (450°F.—Gas Mark 7) for about 20 minutes. Reduce heat after 15 minutes if the cakes are becoming too brown.

Frangipani tarts

cooking time   1½ hours

you will need:

6 oz. puff pastry (see page 64)	2 teaspoons cornflour
	1 dessertspoon sherry or brandy
¾ gill milk	
2 eggs	2 teaspoons chopped peel
3 oz. sugar	grated rind of ½ lemon
chopped nuts	angelica

1 Line fairly deep tartlet tins with the pastry.

2 Blend the cornflour with the milk and put into a saucepan, together with 1 dessertspoon of the sugar, and cook until thickened.

3 Take the pan off the heat and when no longer boiling whisk in the beaten egg yolks and brandy, together with the lemon rind and peel.

4 Put into tartlet cases.

5 Put into the centre of a hot oven (450°F.—Gas Mark 7) and bake for nearly 20 minutes.

6 Take out of the oven, whip the egg whites until very stiff. Fold in nearly all the sugar.

7 Pile or pipe on top of the mixture.

8 While doing this have the oven door wide open so that the heat can be dispersed as quickly as possible.

9 Dust the tops of the tarts with the last of the sugar, sprinkle with nuts and pieces of angelica.

10 Return to the oven at 225°F.—Gas Mark ¼ for about 1 hour.

Hasty doughnuts

cooking time   6–7 minutes

you will need:

8 oz. self-raising flour (with plain flour use 2 teaspoons baking powder)	pinch salt
	1 gill milk
	sugar
	fat for frying
1 egg	

1 Beat ingredients together and drop spoonfuls into hot fat, fry steadily until brown then turn and fry on second side.

2 If you wish to cut ring shapes you will get a better texture by rubbing 1 oz. margarine into the mixture then using slightly less milk so that you can roll out the dough.

3 Drain and roll in castor sugar.

4 Split and fill with jam when cold.

Lemon curd tarts

cooking time   12–15 minutes

you will need:

6 oz. short crust pastry (see page 63)	6–8 oz. lemon curd (see below)

1 Roll out pastry and line approximately 12 patty tins.

2 Prick lightly with a fork to prevent pastry rising in cooking.

3 Either bake the pastry cases 'blind', i.e. with no filling OR put in a little curd.

4 Bake just above the centre of a moderately hot oven—if filling is used—or a hot oven with no filling (400–450°F.—Gas Mark 5–7).

5 Either fill with curd the moment they come from the oven, or add extra curd. Or leave until quite cold then fill with curd.

Lemon curd

cooking time   approximately 45 minutes

you will need:

8 oz. castor or loaf sugar	4 oz. fresh butter or margarine
2 eggs	rind of 3 lemons
	juice of 2 large lemons

1 Grate the rind carefully, removing just the yellow 'zest' but none of the white pith.

2 If using loaf sugar, rub this over the lemons until all the yellow has been removed.

3 Squeeze the juice from the fruit.

4 Put all ingredients (except eggs) into double saucepan or basin over hot water.

5 Cook, stirring from time to time, until all the margarine and sugar have melted.

6 Add the well-beaten eggs.

7 Continue cooking until the mixture coats the back of a wooden spoon.

8 Pour into jars and seal down.

Mixed fruit fingers

cooking time   30 minutes

you will need:

5 oz. margarine	3 oz. sugar
milk to mix	8 oz. flour (preferably plain)
2 oz. glacé cherries	
2 oz. dates	2 oz. chopped nuts
icing sugar	2 oz. sultanas

1 Rub 4 oz. of the margarine into the flour.

2 Add 2 oz. sugar and enough milk to make a firm dough.

3 Roll out half the dough until a neat oblong about ¼ inch thick and put on an ungreased baking tin.

4 Put remainder of margarine and sugar into a saucepan.

5 Heat until margarine has melted, then stir in the cherries, nuts and dates (all cut into small pieces) and the sultanas.

6 Mix well then spread over the dough.

7 Roll out the rest of the dough and cover the filling.

8 Put into the centre of a moderate oven (375°F. —Gas Mark 4) for 25–30 minutes. Mark into fingers while still hot but leave on tin to cool.

9 When cold dust with icing sugar.

Jam tarts

cooking time   12–15 minutes

you will need:

6 oz. short crust pastry (see page 63)	6–8 oz. jam

1 Roll out pastry and line approximately 12 patty tins.

2 Prick lightly to prevent the pastry rising in cooking.

3 Put in a very little jam.

4 Bake for approximately 12–15 minutes just above the middle of a moderately hot oven (400°F.—Gas Mark 5).

5 Remove from tins, and stir in the rest of the jam.

6 This method prevents the jam from boiling out during cooking, but gives the 'cooked' flavour that most people prefer in a jam tart.

7 For a new idea in filling the jam can be mixed with a few fine cake crumbs. In this case use 4 oz. jam, 2 oz. cake crumbs, and fill the tartlet cases BEFORE baking.

8 Golden syrup, mixed with a squeeze of lemon juice and a few breadcrumbs could be used instead of jam.

Economical Japanese cakes

cooking time   30 minutes

you will need:

2 oz. sugar	2 oz. ground almonds
3 oz. flour (with plain flour use ½ teaspoon baking powder)	3 oz. butter little milk or egg yolk to mix
for the decoration	
3 oz. butter	4 oz. icing sugar
1½ teaspoons coffee essence	hazel nuts crisp crumbs

1 Cream the butter and sugar together until light and fluffy.
2 Add the flour, almonds and enough milk to make a firm dough.
3 Roll out until ½ inch thick.
4 Put the dough on to an ungreased baking tin.
5 Place in the centre of a moderate oven (375°F. —Gas Mark 4) for 10 minutes.
6 Take the tin out of the oven and mark into small rounds about 1½ inches in diameter.
7 Replace the tin in the oven and cook for a further 10 minutes.
8 Take out of the oven once more and lift rounds on to a wire sieve. Brown the pieces left over for 10 minutes and use these to make the crumbs.
9 Make the butter icing for the decoration by creaming the butter, sugar and coffee essence. Sandwich 2 of the rounds together with a little butter icing then cover the tops and sides with this icing. Roll in the crisp crumbs. Decorate with a hazel nut.

Macaroon tarts

cooking time   15–20 minutes

you will need:

6 oz. short crust pastry (see page 63)	2 egg whites
4 oz. ground almonds little jam	4 oz. castor sugar few drops almond essence

1 Roll out the pastry, cut into rounds and line patty tins with this.
2 Spread with a small amount of jam.
3 Whisk the egg whites, add the almond essence, ground almonds and sugar.
4 Spread this mixture into the patty cases, lined with pastry, being careful not to put in too much mixture.
5 If any pastry remains, roll very thinly indeed, cut into very narrow strips and make crosses of these on each tart.
6 Bake for approximately 15–20 minutes in the centre of a hot oven (425–450°F.—Gas Mark 6–7).

Variations

For economy use half ground almonds and half semolina or fine cake crumbs.
Use 3 oz. ground almonds and 1 oz. chocolate powder for chocolate macaroons.

Pineapple cream tarts

cooking time   15 minutes

you will need:

6 oz. puff pastry (see page 64)	5 oz. well-drained chopped pineapple
1 gill mock or whipped cream	water icing (see page 82) cherries

1 Line the tartlet tins with the puff pastry.
2 Put a small piece of paper with a crust of bread in each so that they do not rise too much at the bottom.
3 Bake for 15 minutes near the top of a very hot oven (475°F.—Gas Mark 8).
4 Lower the heat after 10 minutes, if the pastry appears to be browning too much.
5 When the tartlets are cold, mix the pineapple and cream together.
6 Fill the tarts with the mixture then cover with a thin layer of water icing.
7 Allow this to set, then decorate with a cherry.

Rice tarts

cooking time   20 minutes

you will need:

6 oz. short crust pastry (see page 63)

filling

2 oz. butter	2 oz. ground rice
2 oz. sugar	1 egg
raspberry jam	little grated lemon rind

1 Line patty tins with pastry and spread with jam.
2 Cream butter and sugar and other ingredients and put on jam.
3 Bake for 20 minutes in hot oven (425–450°F.— Gas Mark 6–7).

Shropshire mint cakes

cooking time   20 minutes

you will need:

8 oz. flaky pastry (see page 63)	6 oz. currants
1 oz. butter	1 oz. crystallized peel
2 oz. castor sugar	1 tablespoon freshly chopped mint

1 Prepare pastry.
2 Mix all of the ingredients together and make as Eccles cakes (see page 70).

Welsh cheesecakes

cooking time   approximately 25–30 minutes

you will need:

4 oz. short crust pastry (see page 63)	1 egg
raspberry jam	2 oz. flour
2 oz. butter	grated rind ½ lemon
2 oz. sugar	pinch baking powder
	little castor sugar

1 Line some patty tins with short crust pastry then put a little raspberry jam into the bottom of each.
2 Beat the butter and sugar together then beat in the egg.
3 Add the flour, lemon rind and lastly the baking powder.
4 Put 1 teaspoon of this mixture over the jam in each patty tin and bake in centre of a moderately hot oven (400°F.—Gas Mark 5) till nicely browned.
5 Cool on a wire tray. Before serving sprinkle with castor sugar.

Walnut griddle cakes

cooking time   10 minutes

you will need:

4 oz. plain flour	2 oz. finest semolina
pinch salt	1 tablespoon castor
3 level teaspoons	sugar
baking powder	2 lightly beaten eggs
2 oz. chopped walnuts	1 gill milk
butter	1 tablespoon melted
maple or golden syrup	butter or margarine

1 Sift flour, baking powder, salt and semolina into a bowl.
2 Add sugar.
3 Make a well in the centre of the mixture and add the eggs and milk.
4 Beat thoroughly to form a thick creamy batter.
5 Stir in melted fat and walnuts.
6 Drop spoonfuls on to a well-greased, heated griddle, thick frying-pan, or hot plate of an electric cooker.
7 Cook till brown on both sides.
8 Serve with butter and maple syrup or golden syrup.

Walnut diamonds

cooking time   20 minutes

you will need:

4 oz. luxury margarine	4 oz. flour (with plain
4 oz. castor sugar	flour 1 level teaspoon
2 eggs	baking powder)
2 oz. chopped walnuts	finely grated rind 1 orange
for frosting and	3 tablespoons orange
decoration	marmalade, heated,
1 egg white	strained and re-heated
walnut halves	

1 Cream together sugar and margarine until light and fluffy.
2 Add eggs one at a time, beating thoroughly after each addition.
3 Stir in orange rind.
4 Lightly fold in sieved flour and walnuts.
5 Place mixture in Swiss roll tin, 11 × 7 inches, well greased and lined with greaseproof paper coming 1 inch above top of tin.
6 Bake on second shelf from top in moderate oven (375°F.—Gas Mark 4) for 20 minutes.
7 Cool on wire tray.
8 Make frosting. Whisk egg white until stiff and peaky, then pour in hot marmalade.
9 Re-whisk until cool and stiff enough for spreading.
10 Spread top of cake with frosting then cut into diamond shapes. Decorate each with half a walnut.

Fruit buns

you will need:

12 oz. plain flour	approximately 1½ gills
good pinch salt	tepid water, milk and
1 oz. margarine or	water, or milk
cooking fat	1–2 oz. sugar
2–4 oz. dried fruit	1 oz. sugar for glaze
1–2 oz. candied peel	1 tablespoon water
½ oz. yeast	

1 Cream the yeast with 1 teaspoon of the sugar.
2 Add the tepid liquid and a sprinkling flour.
3 Put into a warm place until the 'sponge' breaks through.
4 Meanwhile sieve the flour and salt into a warm bowl, rub in the margarine and add the sugar, fruit and peel.
5 When ready, work in the yeast liquid and knead thoroughly.
6 Put into a warm place for approximately 1 hour to 'prove' i.e. until the dough just about doubles its original size.
7 Form into round buns, 'prove' for 15 minutes on warm tray and bake for 10 minutes near the top of a very hot oven (475°F.—Gas Mark 8).
8 Mix the sugar with 1 tablespoon of water and the moment the buns come from the oven, brush with this to give an attractive glaze.

Variations on fruit buns

CHELSEA BUNS. Make up dough *without* fruit and stiff enough to roll into neat oblong after 'proving'. Brush on 1 oz. melted margarine. Over this sprinkle 1 oz. sugar and 2 oz. dried fruit. Roll up, cut into 1–1½ inch portions and 'prove' and bake as fruit buns. When baked either glaze or sprinkle with castor sugar.

SWISS BUNS. Omit fruit, cut into fingers. 'Prove' and bake as fruit buns then coat with water icing.

Chapter 12
Tea Time — Cakes, Gâteaux and Icings

Learning to bake perfectly is something anyone can learn with a little care and patience. Even if you have had no experience in baking, if you follow my tips for easy baking to the letter, you should have no difficulty in making any one of the delicious cakes in this chapter – whether it is a simple sponge or one of the more elaborate gâteaux.

10 tips for easy baking

1 Follow the recipe exactly for the first time, then you can modify or alter it slightly afterwards if you wish.
2 Weigh your ingredients carefully, and choose the best quality you can afford.
3 In sponge and light cakes take care not to over-beat the flour.
4 Try and keep all things you are using at the same temperature.
5 Where possible use tins that are the same size as the recipe states. If you have to use smaller, then your cake will take longer to bake, if larger, then the cake will be cooked in a shorter time.
6 Remember that every oven is different and the temperatures given in recipes are just a guide. Your knowledge of the oven you use, plus the manufacturer's instructions, are the important things to follow.
7 Learn the right way to test whether a cake is baked. First press firmly but gently, in the centre. If 'springy' it is fairly safe to bring it out of the oven. If your finger leaves an impression, your cake is not cooked.
8 To test a rich fruit cake—listen. If the cake makes a distinct humming sound, it is not quite cooked.
9 Cool cakes away from draughts, and when quite cold, put into air-tight tins away from biscuits, bread or pastry.
10 Never use damp fruit, always wash 48 hours before you need it.

To make cakes that keep well

If you wish cakes to keep for any length of time there are certain things that are important to remember:

1 A certain amount of golden syrup or treacle is a great help.
2 A high percentage of fruit in the recipe keeps cakes moist.
3 Some of the uncooked cakes of today keep well in refrigerators.
4 Meringue or meringue-type cakes keep well. Store separately from other cakes.
5 A very rich biscuit-type of cake keeps well.
6 In order to keep cakes at their best they should never be put with bread, pastry or biscuits.
7 In order to store rich biscuits well never put into the same tin as chocolate biscuits.

Ripon apple cake

cooking time   30 minutes

1 Line a tin with short crust pastry, cover with *thinly* sliced cooking apples and plenty of sugar.
2 Cover with a thin layer of grated cheese, then more pastry.
3 Bake for about 30 minutes in the centre of a moderately hot oven (400°F.—Gas Mark 5).

Cherry almond loaf

cooking time $1\frac{1}{2}$ hours

you will need:

5 oz. margarine or butter	6 oz. flour (with plain
2 oz. ground almonds	flour use $1\frac{1}{2}$ level
4 oz. glacé cherries	teaspoon baking
2 large eggs	powder)
marzipan or water icing	few drops milk
(optional)	almonds and cherries
6 oz. castor sugar	(to decorate)

1 Halve and flour the cherries (or wash off the sticky syrup, dry well and flour).
2 Cream together margarine and sugar.
3 Add the beaten eggs, sieved flour and the ground almonds.
4 Stir in the cherries and enough milk to give a stiff consistency.
5 Put into a loaf tin and bake for approximately $1\frac{1}{2}$ hours in the centre of a very slow oven (300°F.—Gas Mark 2).
6 Turn out carefully.
7 If wished cover the top with either marzipan or water icing and decorate with blanched almonds and cherries.
8 The slow baking of this cake produces a lovely moist texture.

Economical chocolate cake

cooking time   30 minutes

you will need:

1 oz. cocoa	1 gill milk
3 oz. margarine	5 oz. castor sugar
1 egg	5 oz. self-raising flour
2 oz. bar of chocolate	few drops vanilla essence
chopped nuts	grated chocolate

1 Boil together the cocoa, milk and 2 oz. of the castor sugar.
2 Allow the mixture to cool.
3 Cream together the rest of the sugar and the margarine.
4 Add 1 beaten egg and a few drops vanilla essence.
5 Sieve the flour.
6 Stir the cocoa liquid and the flour alternately into the creamed margarine until smooth and soft.
7 Line the bottom of a 9-inch sandwich tin with greased paper, put in this mixture and bake for approximately 30 minutes (375°F.—Gas Mark 4) until firm and 'spongy'.
8 When the cake is cold, melt a 2 oz. bar of chocolate in a basin over hot water, adding 2 teaspoons hot water to the chocolate.
9 Spread over the cake and allow to harden.
10 Decorate with chopped nuts and grated chocolate.

Coconut cake

cooking time   1¼ hours

you will need:

5 oz. butter or margarine	5 oz. castor sugar
2 eggs	6 oz. flour (with plain flour use 2 level teaspoons baking powder)
2 oz. dessicated coconut	
little milk	
little jam }	
coconut } to	
cherries } decorate	

1 Cream butter and sugar.
2 Beat in the eggs.
3 Stir in the sieved flour and dessicated coconut with enough milk to make a sticky consistency i.e. so that the mixture only drops from the spoon when shaken very hard.
4 Put into a greased and floured loaf tin and bake for approximately 1¼ hours in the centre of a very moderate oven (350°F.—Gas Mark 3). When cold spread with jam, sprinkle with coconut and decorate with cherries.

Curd cake

cooking time   20–30 minutes

you will need:

6 oz. flaky pastry (see page 63)	1–2 oz. butter or margarine
1 large or 2 small eggs	the curds from 1 pint of sour milk
2 oz. dried fruit	2 oz. sugar
pinch salt	grating of nutmeg

1 To obtain the curds pour the sour milk into a muslin bag and allow to drip for several hours.
2 Cream the margarine and sugar together.
3 Add the curds, then the well-beaten eggs, the salt and dried fruit.
4 Line a deep pie plate or 12 patty tins with the pastry and pour in the filling.
5 Sprinkle on top with grated nutmeg and put into a hot oven (450°F.—Gas Mark 7) and bake for 10–15 minutes, then lower the heat to moderately hot (400°F.—Gas Mark 5) for a further 10–15 minutes.

Family currant cake

cooking time   1¼–1½ hours

you will need:

8 oz. flour (with plain flour use 3 level teaspoons baking powder)	4 oz. margarine or cooking fat
	6 oz. currants
	4 oz. castor sugar
pinch salt	1 egg
	5 tablespoons milk

1 Sieve the flour, salt and baking powder (if used) into a basin.
2 Rub in the margarine until the mixture is as fine as breadcrumbs.
3 Add the cleaned fruit and sugar and mix well.
4 Beat the egg and add the milk and mix with the dry ingredients to a consistency that will drop from the spoon.
5 Grease a 2-lb. loaf tin or a 6-inch cake tin.
6 Turn the mixture into the prepared cake tin and bake in the middle of a moderate oven (375°F.—Gas Mark 4) for 1–1¼ hours for loaf tin and 1¼–1½ hours for round tin.

Rock buns

The above mixture can be used for rock buns or currant buns. For rock buns use mixed fruit. Use only 1–2 tablespoons milk, put the mixture into 'heaps' on well greased baking tins, allowing room to spread out. Bake for approximately 10 minutes near the top of a hot oven (450°F.—Gas Mark 7).

The mixture can be dusted with sugar before baking to give a glaze.

Economical luncheon cake

Use mixed fruit and 1–2 oz. mixed peel. Bake in a loaf tin.

Date and ginger cake

cooking time   50–60 minutes

you will need:

4 oz. margarine
2 level tablespoons
  golden syrup
½ level teaspoon
  bicarbonate of soda
just under ½ gill milk
  or water
1 egg
3 oz. sugar

4 oz. chopped dates
  (use the block dates)
7 oz. self-raising flour
  (with plain flour use
  1½ level teaspoons
  baking powder)
1 teaspoon powdered
  ginger

1 Melt the margarine, sugar and golden syrup in a pan.
2 Sieve dry ingredients.
3 Add the melted ingredients, the dates, egg, and beat well.
4 Heat the milk in the pan for 1 minute (this saves wasting any syrup etc.), pour over the flour mixture and beat well.
5 Put into a well-greased and floured tin. An oblong tin similar to that used for a gingerbread is excellent, otherwise use a 7-inch round tin.
6 Bake for about 50–60 minutes in the centre of a very moderate oven (350°F.—Gas Mark 3).
7 Allow a little longer in the 7-inch round tin.

Peach spice cake

cooking time   25–30 minutes

you will need:

6 oz. flour (with plain
  flour 1½ level
  teaspoons
  baking powder)
6 oz. butter or
  margarine

3 medium eggs
large pinch salt
2 level teaspoons mixed
  spice
1 level teaspoon cinnamon
6 oz. castor sugar

vanilla cream

6 oz. butter or
  margarine
12 oz. icing sugar,
  sieved

1 teaspoon vanilla
  essence
2 tablespoons milk

decoration

6 peach halves,
  drained of syrup

1 oz. walnuts, finely
  chopped

1 Sift together dry ingredients.
2 Cream fat and sugar till light and fluffy then add eggs, 1 at a time, beating thoroughly after each addition.
3 Fold in dry ingredients then divide mixture equally between 2 well greased 8-inch sandwich tins.
4 Bake just above centre of a moderate oven (375°F.—Gas Mark 4) for 25–30 minutes.
5 Turn out on to a wire tray and leave till cold.

Vanilla Cream

1 Beat fat and vanilla essence till soft then gradually stir in the sugar alternately with the milk.
2 Cream well till mixture is light, fluffy and smooth.
3 Split each cake in half then sandwich layers together with vanilla cream.

4 Spread remainder over top and sides of cake then press walnuts against the sides.
5 Arrange peach halves on top then decorate with small teaspoons of vanilla cream.
6 Chill before serving.

Good Dundee cake

cooking time   approximately 2–2¼ hours

you will need:

6 oz. margarine or
  butter
6 oz. sugar
8 oz. plain flour
1½ level teaspoons
  baking powder
3 eggs
1 lb. mixed dried fruit

2 oz. chopped almonds or
  ground almonds
2 oz. split almonds
2 oz. cherries
2 oz. peel
2 tablespoons milk
1 teaspoon spice

1 Cream the margarine and sugar together until soft and light.
2 Add the beaten eggs.
3 Sieve dry ingredients together.
4 Chop a few of the almonds and split the others.
5 Mix the chopped almonds, floured cherries, fruit and peel together.
6 Stir in the flour and enough milk to make a slow dropping consistency, then lastly put in the fruit.
7 Put into a greased and floured 8-inch cake tin.
8 Cover with the split almonds and brush with a little egg white to glaze.
9 Bake for 2–2¼ hours in the centre of a very moderate oven (325–350°F.—Gas Mark 3) reducing the heat after 1½ hours if wished.
10 Cool slightly in tin before turning on to wire sieve.

Boiled fruit cake

(An exceptionally economical cake that does not dry easily)

cooking time   1½ hours

you will need:

10 oz. flour (if using
  plain flour add 3
  level teaspoons
  baking powder)
1 teaspoon mixed spice
pinch salt

1 teaspoon bicarbonate
  of soda
½ pint water or
  preferably cold tea
3 oz. fat
3 oz. sugar
3 oz. dried fruit

1 Boil the liquid, fat, sugar and fruit together in a pan for 2 or 3 minutes.
2 Allow to cool slightly.
3 Meanwhile, sieve together the dry ingredients.
4 Add the liquid and beat thoroughly.
5 Pour into a greased and floured 8-inch cake tin.
6 Bake in the centre of a moderately hot oven (400°F.—Gas Mark 5) for 45 minutes, then lower the heat to Gas Mark 4 or reduce the heat to 375°F. for a further 30–45 minutes.

1-egg fruit cake

cooking time   approximately 1–1½ hours depending on tin

you will need:

5 oz. margarine or 3 oz. margarine and 2 oz. lard	1 egg
	6 oz. mixed dried fruit
4–5 oz. sugar	2 oz. mixed peel
8 oz. flour (with plain flour use 2 level teaspoons baking powder)	1 oz. almonds (not essential)
	1 dessertspoon cherries (not essential)
	little milk

1 Sieve flour and baking powder together.
2 Rub in margarine, add sugar, dried fruit and peel, then the beaten egg and enough milk to make a sticky consistency.
3 Put into a well greased and floured loaf tin and bake for just 1–1¼ hours in the centre of a moderate oven (350–375°F.—Gas Mark 3–4).
4 If using the almonds and cherries blanch and dry the almonds then put on top of the cake with the halved cherries, before baking.
5 If using 6-inch round cake tin allow 1¼–1½ hours at 350°F.—Gas Mark 3.
6 **Variations:** Omit the dried fruit and add 3–4 oz. chopped and lightly floured cherries.
Add the finely grated rind and juice of 1 large orange, omitting some of the milk.
Omit the dried fruit and increase the peel from 2 to 5 oz.

Rich rock buns

This mixture can also be used for rich rock buns. Be very careful when adding the milk, a few drops only will be needed. Put into small 'heaps' on well greased tins, allowing room to spread out. Bake for a good 10 minutes near the top of a hot oven (450°F.—Gas Mark 7). Cool slightly on the tins, before removing, since the cakes are inclined to be brittle. Sugar can be shaken over the cakes BEFORE baking to give a glaze.

Eggless fruit cake

cooking time   2¼ hours

you will need:

8 oz. flour (with plain flour use 1½ level teaspoons baking powder)	1 teaspoon spice
	12 oz. mixed dried fruit
	3 oz. margarine
1 teaspoon bicarbonate of soda	3 oz. sugar
	2 oz. mixed peel
	1 gill milk

1 Cream the margarine and sugar until soft.
2 Sieve flour, soda, baking powder and spice.
3 Work into margarine together with milk.
4 Lastly add the fruit and peel.
5 Leave in bowl overnight.
6 Next day stir again and put into 8-inch cake tin lined with greased and floured paper.
7 Bake for 2¼ hours in the middle of a very moderate oven (350°F.—Gas Mark 3).

Fruit shortcake

cooking time   15 minutes

you will need:

4 oz. margarine	6 oz. flour (with plain flour use 1½ level teaspoon baking powder)
4 oz. sugar	
1 egg	
fruit and cream	very little milk if needed

1 Cream together margarine and sugar until soft and white.
2 Add the egg and the flour.
3 Mix thoroughly and if the mixture does not bind add a few drops only of milk.
4 Divide the mixture in half, form into neat rounds and put into two well-greased and floured 6- or 7-inch sandwich tins, pressing flat with damp fingers.
5 Bake for just about 15 minutes near the top of a moderately hot oven (425°F.—Gas Mark 6).
6 Allow to cool for a few minutes before turning out, then cool.
7 After the cakes are cold sandwich together with cream and sliced fruit and top with whole fruit and cream.

Gingerbread

cooking time   1–1¼ hours

you will need:

4 oz. butter or margarine or fat	7 oz. flour (with plain flour use 2 level teaspoons baking powder)
6 oz. black treacle or golden syrup	
4 oz. brown sugar	2 teaspoons powdered ginger
3 tablespoons water	
	1 egg

1 Put the butter, sugar and treacle into pan and heat gently, until the butter has melted.
2 Sieve all the dry ingredients on to the wet mixture and beat hard until thoroughly mixed.
3 Make sure no mixture is left in pan.
4 Add the egg.
5 Heat water in pan and pour over flour mixture.
6 Beat once again, then pour into tin lined with paper.
7 If using a 7-inch round cake tin bake for 1–1¼ hours in the centre of a very moderate oven (350°F.—Gas Mark 3). An oblong tin will take just under 1 hour.
8 Test by pressing gently in the centre of the cake.
9 If no impression is left by your finger the cake is cooked.
10 Cool for about 30 minutes in the tin, then turn out carefully on to a wire sieve.

Variations

Almond gingerbread. Use 6 oz. flour and 1 oz. ground almonds. Cover with water icing and browned almonds.
Lemon gingerbread. Add grated rind of 1 lemon and 1 tablespoon lemon juice and 2 tablespoons water.

Economical Madeira cake

cooking time   1¼ hours

you will need:

4 oz. margarine	1 teaspoon grated
4 oz. castor sugar	lemon rind
8 oz. flour (with plain	milk to mix
flour use 2 level	little sugar
teaspoons baking	piece candied lemon peel
powder)	for top of cake
2 eggs	

1 Cream together the margarine and sugar until soft and light.
2 Sieve flour and baking powder together.
3 Beat eggs.
4 Add eggs and flour alternately to margarine mixture, with lemon rind and enough milk to make a soft consistency.
5 Put into greased and floured 7-inch cake tin, sprinkling a little sugar on top and putting on the piece of lemon peel.
6 Bake for approximately 1¼ hours in the middle of a moderate oven (375°F.—Gas Mark 4).

Variations

Cherry Cake: Add 4 oz. chopped floured glacé cherries.
Genoa Cake: Add 4–6 oz. mixed dried fruit.

Rich Madeira cake

cooking time   1½–1¾ hours

you will need:

6 oz. butter	3 eggs and very little milk
6 oz. castor sugar	OR
8 oz. flour (with plain	4 eggs and no milk
flour use 2 level	little sugar
teaspoons baking	piece candied lemon peel
powder)	for top of cake

1 Method as for economical Madeira cake (see above) but bake for 1½–1¾ hours in centre of very moderate oven (350°F.—Gas Mark 3).

Variations

Seed Cake: Add ½–1 tablespoon caraway seeds.
Coconut Cake: Use 6 oz. flour, 2 oz. desiccated coconut.

Crisp orange coconut cake

cooking time   45–50 minutes

you will need:

4 oz. margarine	3 tablespoons orange
4 oz. castor sugar	juice
2 eggs	6 oz. flour (with plain
grated rind of 1 orange	flour 1½ level
	teaspoons baking
	powder)

topping

1½ oz. margarine	1½ oz. desiccated coconut
1½ oz. brown sugar	1 tablespoon orange juice

1 Cream the margarine and sugar together until light and fluffy.
2 Beat in the orange rind, add the eggs, 1 at a time and beat well.
3 Fold in the sieved flour, alternately with the orange juice.
4 Put into a greased 8- or 9-inch sandwich tin.
5 Bake just above centre of a moderate oven (375°F.—Gas Mark 4) for 35–40 minutes.

Topping

6 Cream margarine, brown sugar and coconut with the orange juice and spread evenly over the cake. Grill *gently* until golden brown. Cool on a cake rack.

Moist orange cake

cooking time   50 minutes

you will need:

6 oz. flour (with plain	pinch salt
flour use 2 level	2 teaspoons grated
teaspoons baking	orange rind
powder)	3 oz. sugar
1 or 2 eggs	2 good tablespoons
2 oz. butter, margarine	marmalade
or cooking fat	¼ gill boiling water (or
1 level teaspoon	use water and orange
bicarbonate of soda	juice)

1 Sieve all the dry ingredients together into a mixing bowl.
2 Melt the fat, marmalade and sugar in a pan.
3 Pour on to dry ingredients, beating well.
4 Add the eggs and lastly boiling water.
5 Beat the cake mixture until bubbles appear on the surface.
6 Pour into a tin lined with greased paper. If using one measuring 7 inches by 4 inches, bake for exactly 50 minutes in the centre of a very moderate oven (350°F.—Gas Mark 3).
7 Allow to cool for about 30 minutes in the tin before turning on to a wire sieve.
8 Try to keep this cake 2 or 3 days before cutting since the flavour will improve.

Moist lemon cake

Recipe as for moist orange cake but use lemons in place of oranges and lemon marmalade when available.

Rich plain cake

cooking time   1½ hours

you will need:

8 oz. butter (or margarine)	8 oz. castor sugar
5 eggs (or use 4 eggs and 2 tablespoons milk)	10 oz. flour (with plain flour use 2½ level teaspoons baking powder)
2 oz. ground almonds—helps to keep the cake moist	icing sugar (for garnish)

This 8-inch cake will keep beautifully for some days. For a 5-inch cake use half quantities and bake for just over half the cooking time.

1 Cream together the butter and sugar until soft and light.
2 Beat the eggs and add gradually to the butter mixture.
3 Sieve the flour, mix with the ground almonds and stir gently into the butter mixture.
4 Grease and flour an 8-inch cake tin, put in the mixture.
5 If your tin is not a very good one it is worthwhile lining it with greased greaseproof paper.
6 Bake in the centre of a very moderate oven (325–350°F.—Gas Mark 3) for approximately 1½ hours.
7 Dust the top with sieved icing sugar.

Pineapple cake

Add a few drops of pineapple essence to the cake mixture, and, if possible, omit 1 oz. of flour and add 1 oz. of pineapple-flavoured blancmange powder. Omit the ground almonds and add instead 2 oz. chopped crystallized pineapple.

Ginger and almond cake

Use the rich plain cake, but add 2 oz. chopped blanched almonds instead of ground almonds. Sieve ½–1 teaspoon powdered ginger with the flour and add 2–3 oz. finely chopped crystallized ginger. When the cake is cold it can be covered with water icing and decorated with slices of crystallized ginger and blanched almonds.

Vinegar fruit cake

cooking time   1½ hours

you will need:

12 oz. self-raising flour	6 oz. sugar
½ pint milk	1 teaspoon bicarbonate of soda
6 oz. fat	8 oz. fruit
2 tablespoons vinegar	

1 Rub the fat into the flour.
2 Add sugar and fruit.
3 Stir the bicarbonate of soda and vinegar into the milk and add to the other ingredients.
4 Put mixture into a greased and floured tin.
5 Bake in the centre of a moderate oven for approximately 1½ hours (350–375°F.—Gas Mark 3–4).

One-egg sponge

cooking time   15–18 minutes

you will need:

1 oz. margarine	4 oz. flour (with plain flour use 2 level teaspoons baking powder)
1 egg	
¼ teaspoon bicarbonate of soda	
1 tablespoon warmed golden syrup	½ gill milk or milk and water
3 oz. sugar	

1 Cream together the margarine, sugar and syrup.
2 Add the egg and flour alternately to the fat mixture.
3 If using baking powder this should be sifted with the flour.
4 Dissolve the bicarbonate of soda in the milk and lastly, beat this into the mixture.
5 Pour into two 6-inch greased and floured sandwich tins and bake on second shelf from top of a hot oven (450°F.—Gas Mark 7) for approximately 15–18 minutes.

Sponge sandwich (whisking method)

cooking time   10–12 minutes

you will need:

3 large eggs—at least day old	1 oz. melted butter or margarine—if cake is to be kept for day or two
3 oz. flour (½ level teaspoon baking powder can be added with plain flour)	1 tablespoon hot water
	jam (for filling)
4 oz. castor sugar	castor sugar (for top)

1 Put the eggs and sugar into a basin and whisk hard until thick.
2 You will get a lighter result if *not* whisked over hot water.
3 FOLD in the well-sieved flour carefully and gently with a metal spoon.
4 FOLD in water and margarine or butter.
5 Grease and flour, or grease, and coat with equal quantities of flour and sugar two 7-inch sandwich tins.
6 Divide the mixture between them and bake for 10–12 minutes near the top of really hot oven. With gas it is a good idea to heat the oven on 8 then turn to 6 or 7 when cakes go in.
7 With electricity heat to 450–475°F. then re-set oven to 425°F. when cakes go in.
8 Test by pressing gently but firmly in the centre of the cakes.
9 When firm they are cooked.
10 Take out of oven, leave for 1 minute, tap tins sharply then turn on to a sieve.
11 *Cool away from a draught.*
12 Sandwich together with jam and dust on top with sieved icing sugar.

For a chocolate sponge

Omit $\frac{1}{2}$ oz. flour, add $\frac{1}{2}$ oz. cocoa, or omit 1 oz. flour and use $1\frac{1}{2}$ oz. drinking chocolate powder instead. Fill with whipped cream, cover with icing sugar or chocolate icing (see page 82).

Ginger sponge sandwich

cooking time   17 minutes approximately

you will need:

4 oz. margarine or butter	4 oz. castor sugar
2 large eggs	4 oz. self-raising flour (or plain flour and
1 level teaspoon powdered ginger	1 teaspoon of baking powder)
good pinch mixed spice	grated rind of 1 lemon

butter icing

2 oz. butter	3 oz. icing sugar
$\frac{1}{2}$ teaspoon lemon rind	$\frac{1}{2}$ teaspoon powdered
2 oz. crystallized ginger	ginger

to decorate
2 oz. crystallized ginger

1 Cream together margarine (or butter) and sugar until soft and light.
2 Add the beaten eggs and the sieved dry ingredients alternately.
3 Lastly add the lemon rind.
4 Put into 2 6-inch greased and floured tins and bake for about 17 minutes near the top of a moderately hot oven (375–400°F.—Gas Mark 4–5).
5 Sandwich together with the butter icing.
6 Cream together butter and sieved icing sugar.
7 Add $\frac{1}{2}$ teaspoon grated lemon rind and $\frac{1}{2}$ teaspoon powdered ginger.
8 Chop 2 oz. crystallized ginger (or well drained stem ginger) and mix into half the filling.
9 Spread this between the cakes and then swirl rest of plain butter icing on top.
10 Decorate with pieces of ginger.

Golden sponge sandwich

cooking time   17 minutes

you will need:

3 oz. margarine	4 oz. castor sugar
1 oz. golden syrup	2 large eggs
4 oz. self-raising flour (with plain flour use 1 teaspoon baking powder)	1 level teaspoon powdered ginger or mixed spice
spiced butter filling	grated rind of lemon
	good pinch mixed spice

1 Cream together margarine, syrup and sugar until soft and light.
2 Add the beaten eggs and the sieved dry ingredients alternately, taking care not to overbeat.
3 Lastly add the lemon rind.
4 Put into two 6-inch greased and floured tins and bake for about 17 minutes near top of a moderately hot oven (375–400°F.—Gas Mark 4–5).
5 Keep wrapped in foil until ready to ice. Turn

out and sandwich together and decorate with this filling.

Spiced butter filling

2 oz. margarine	$\frac{1}{2}$ teaspoon powdered
$\frac{1}{2}$ teaspoon grated lemon rind	ginger or mixed spice
3 oz. sieved icing sugar	3–4 oz. crystallized ginger (or well-drained stem ginger)

Cream margarine and sugar and all other ingredients.

Swiss roll

cooking time   9–10 minutes

you will need:

3 eggs	3 oz. flour (with plain
4 oz. castor sugar	flour use $\frac{1}{2}$ teaspoon
fresh or butter cream for filling or jam	baking powder)

1 Whisk the eggs and sugar until thick, light and fluffy.
2 Carefully fold in the sieved flour.
3 Pour into a large greased and lined Swiss roll tin.
4 Bake near top of hot oven (425–450°F.—Gas Mark 6–7) for about 9–10 minutes. When cooked turn at once on to a piece of sugared greaseproof paper. Trim the edges with a sharp knife. Spread with warm jam.
5 If using cream filling carefully roll up so that the greaseproof paper is rolled inside.
6 Allow to cool and then gently unroll.
7 Remove the paper.
8 Spread evenly with cream or filling and roll up again.
9 Sprinkle with castor sugar.
10 For a smaller Swiss roll use 2 eggs, $2\frac{3}{4}$ oz. sugar, 2 oz. flour.
11 For a chocolate Swiss roll use $2\frac{1}{2}$ oz. flour, $\frac{1}{2}$ oz. cocoa, sieved well together, and fill with cream or butter icing (see page 82).

Victoria sandwich

cooking time   approximately 20 minutes

you will need:

6 oz. flour (with plain flour use $1\frac{1}{2}$ level teaspoons baking powder)	6 oz. castor sugar
	3 eggs (if the eggs are unusually small, allow 1 dessertspoon water per egg to make up the extra liquid)
6 oz. margarine or butter	

1 Sieve flour and baking powder together.
2 Cream the margarine and sugar until soft and white.
3 Break the eggs into a cup to ensure each one is good before beating thoroughly in a basin.
4 Add a little of the beaten egg to the margarine mixture and stir carefully.
5 Add a little flour and stir gently.

6 Continue in this way, adding egg and flour alternately until thoroughly mixed or beat in all eggs then add flour.

7 Grease and flour the two 7-inch sandwich tins carefully and divide the mixture equally between them.

8 Spread slightly away from the centre so that the 2 halves will be flat.

9 Bake for a good 20 minutes in a moderate oven (375–400°F.—Gas Mark 4–5).

10 Using gas oven either put the tins side by side on a shelf just about 2 rungs from the top of the oven or put one under the other.

11 With electric oven or solid fuel put one about the second rung from the top and one the second rung from the bottom or have tins side by side on same shelf.

12 Test by pressing gently but firmly on top and if no impression is left by the finger the cake is ready to come out of the oven.

13 Turn out of the tins on to a wire sieve.

14 It is quite a good idea to give the tins a sharp tap on the table before attempting to turn out the cakes, so loosening the cake away from the sides and bottom of the tin.

15 For 1 cake bake in centre of very moderate oven (350°F.—Gas Mark 3) for approximately 50–60 minutes.

Variations

Chocolate sandwich. Use 5 oz. flour, 1 oz. cocoa. Fill with chocolate butter icing and top with chocolate glacé icing (see page 82).

Coffee sandwich. Use 3 small eggs and 1 good tablespoon coffee essence or 1 teaspoon soluble coffee and 1 tablespoon water. Fill with coffee butter icing and top with coffee butter or glacé icing (see page 82).

Lemon sandwich. Add finely grated rind of 1 or 2 lemons when creaming margarine and sugar. Fill with lemon butter icing and top with lemon glacé or butter icing (see page 82).

Orange sandwich. Add finely grated rind of 1 or 2 oranges when creaming margarine and sugar. Fill with orange butter icing and top with orange glacé or butter icing (see page 82).

Banana cake

cooking time   35 minutes

you will need:

1 large banana	4 oz. self-raising flour
3 oz. castor sugar	(with plain flour use
3 oz. margarine	1 level teaspoon
1 large egg	baking powder)
squeeze of lemon juice	

for the icing

6 tablespoons icing sugar	10 drops lemon juice or water

1 Cream the margarine, sugar and mashed banana well.

2 Add the few drops of lemon juice.

3 Beat in the egg.

4 Fold in the sieved flour.

5 Put into an 8-inch greased and floured sandwich tin (a rather deep one is needed).

6 Bake for approximately 35 minutes in a moderate oven (375°F.—Gas Mark 4).

7 When cold, cover with icing made by mixing the icing sugar with a few drops lemon juice and a little water.

Fudge cake

cooking time $1\frac{1}{4}$ hours

you will need:

4 oz. margarine	4 oz. self-raising flour
2 LEVEL tablespoons golden syrup	(with plain flour add 1 level teaspoon
2 small eggs	baking powder)
2 oz. sugar	

1 Cream margarine, sugar and golden syrup together.

2 Sieve flour.

3 Beat the eggs.

4 Stir the eggs and flour alternately into the creamed margarine.

5 Put into a greased and floured 6-inch cake tin and bake for about $1\frac{1}{4}$ hours in the centre of a very moderate oven (350°F.—Gas Mark 3).

Fudge icing

cooking time   10 minutes

Put 4 oz. white or brown sugar and 1 gill milk into a pan and stir over a steady heat until the sugar has dissolved, then add 1 oz. margarine or butter and a few drops vanilla essence. Boil steadily, stirring from time to time, until the mixture forms a soft ball when tested in cold water (238°F.). Beat slightly, then pour over the cake.

Coffee walnut cake

cooking time   1 hour

you will need:

4 oz. margarine or butter	4 oz. castor sugar
1 tablespoon coffee essence	1 dessertspoon golden syrup
2 oz. chopped walnuts	2 eggs
coffee butter icing	4 oz. flour (with plain
few halved walnuts to decorate	flour use 1 level tea-spoon baking powder)

1 Cream margarine with sugar and syrup until light and fluffy.

2 Add coffee essence.

3 Add slightly whisked eggs in tablespoonfuls, beating mixture well before adding more egg.

4 Sieve flour and fold in together with chopped walnuts.

5 Turn into a 7-inch tin and bake just above centre of a very moderate oven (350°F.—Gas Mark 3) for about 1 hour.

6 Split and fill with coffee butter icing.

Coffee butter icing

Cream 2 oz. margarine, add 4 oz. sieved icing sugar, 2 teaspoons coffee essence and 1 teaspoon milk. Beat well. Sandwich the cake with about ⅔ of this mixture, spread top of cake with remainder. Decorate with halved walnuts.

American frosting

you will need:

6 oz. loaf or granulated sugar	1 egg white
½ gill water	pinch cream of tartar

This is the boiled type of icing that never becomes too hard. It is brittle and crisp on the outside but far softer inside than a royal icing. It is not suitable for piping, but keeps very well on a cake.

1 Put the sugar and water into a saucepan and stir until the sugar has dissolved.

2 Boil steadily until mixture reaches soft ball stage, i.e. when a little is dropped into cold water it forms a soft, pliable ball (238°F.).

3 Beat until the syrup turns cloudy.

4 Pour on to the *stiffly beaten* egg white, adding the cream of tartar.

5 Continue beating until the mixture thickens.

6 Spread on the cake.

7 Pick up at intervals to form peaks on top of the cake.

8 For top only of 7- or 8-inch cake use recipe above. For top and sides of 7- or 8-inch cake use double quantity.

Water icing or Glacé icing

you will need:

8 oz. icing sugar	approximately 1½ dessertspoons warm water

1 To cover the top of a 6-inch sponge use 4 oz. icing sugar; for a 7-inch cake or sponge 6 oz. and for an 8- to 9-inch sponge 8 oz.

2 If covering top and sides use at least double quantities.

3 If the icing sugar seems rather lumpy you can sieve it, but if you add the water and let it stand for some time, unless the lumps are very hard indeed, it will become smooth by itself.

4 Add the water gradually.

Chocolate glacé icing. Add 1 good dessertspoon cocoa to the icing and then beat in a knob of melted butter about the size of an acorn.

Coffee glacé icing. Mix with strong coffee instead of water or with soluble coffee powder, blended with little warm water.

Lemon glacé icing. Mix with lemon juice instead of water.

Orange glacé icing. Mix with orange juice instead of water.

Vanilla glacé icing. Add a few drops of vanilla essence.

Mocha glacé icing. Add 1 good dessertspoon cocoa to the icing sugar and use strong coffee instead of water. A small knob of butter, melted, can be added if wished.

Spiced glacé icing. Blend ½ teaspoon mixed spice, ½ teaspoon grated nutmeg and ½ teaspoon cinnamon with the icing sugar.

Almond glacé icing. Add a few drops of almond essence.

Butter icing

you will need:

2 oz. butter	sugar (to make a firmer icing use the larger quantity of sugar)
flavouring as individual recipe	
3–4 oz. sieved icing	

1 Cream the butter until very soft and white. It is essential not to warm it.

2 Work in the sugar and flavouring.

Chocolate icing. Add good dessertspoon chocolate powder or 1 oz. melted chocolate and few drops vanilla essence.

Coffee icing. Work in good dessertspoon coffee essence or 1 teaspoon soluble coffee powder dissolved in 2 teaspoons water. Do this gradually or mixture will curdle.

Lemon icing. Add 2 teaspoons finely grated lemon rind and gradually beat in 1 dessertspoon lemon juice.

Orange icing. Use 3 teaspoons finely grated orange rind and gradually beat in 1 dessertspoon orange juice.

Rum icing. Add a few drops rum essence or about 1 dessertspoon rum.

Vanilla icing. Add ½ teaspoon vanilla essence to icing.

Royal icing

For top only of 7-inch cake—one layer and little piping.

you will need:

8 oz. sieved icing sugar	1 dessertspoon lemon juice
1 egg white	

1 Whisk the egg whites lightly.

2 Stir in the icing sugar and lemon juice.

3 *Beat well* until very white and smooth.

4 To economise on egg white and to give a somewhat softer icing, omit some of the egg white and use water instead.

5 OR add 1 teaspoon glycerine to each 8 oz. icing sugar.

Marzipan

This is enough for a medium-thick layer on top of a 6–7-inch cake, For an 8–9-inch cake use 6 oz. of ground almonds, etc. For the sides of a cake use at least double quantities and preferably a little more.

you will need:

4 oz. ground almonds	2 oz. castor sugar
2 oz. icing sugar	few drops almond essence
egg yolk to mix	

1 Mix all the ingredients together, adding enough egg yolk to make a firm mixture.

2 Knead thoroughly.

Chapter 13

Light Supper Snacks; Salads, Salad Dressings and Savoury Biscuits

Most families have one main meal and one lighter meal each day, and the recipes following are equally suitable for supper or luncheon. In addition to those contained in this chapter you will find the omelettes in the breakfast section, and some of the recipes in the section on vegetables are good light snacks. Although termed a 'snack' a well balanced meal should have a protein basis—and egg and cheese are ideal for this.

You will also find a number of recipes for salads and salad dressings. Don't serve salads just in summertime, remember when lettuce is expensive that shredded cabbage will take its place very well indeed. A salad blends well with many hot dishes, particularly roast chicken, grilled or fried steak or chips.

Celery rolls

cooking time   approximately 25 minutes

you will need:

½ pint cheese sauce (see page 90)	1 large head celery
cooked macaroni or creamed potatoes	4 thin large slices ham
	little grated cheese

1 Wash the celery and divide the centre into 4 thick pieces.

2 Cook these until just soft in boiling salted water.

3 Drain and wrap each in a slice of ham.

4 Put on to a bed of cooked macaroni or potato, cover with a cheese sauce, grated cheese and brown under the grill.

5 Decorate the edge of the dish with more cooked macaroni.

Cheese pastry

you will need:

short crust pastry made with 8 oz. flour, 4 oz. fat, seasoning and water to mix	4 oz. grated cheese

1 Prepare the short crust pastry in the usual way (see page 63).

2 Roll out to an oblong shape and cover ⅔ of this with half the grated cheese.

3 Fold as for flaky pastry, re-roll and repeat the process with the rest of the cheese.

4 Roll again and cut as required.

Cheese pudding

cooking time   30–40 minutes

you will need:

4–5 oz. grated cheese	4 oz. white bread
2 oz. butter	seasoning
¾ pint milk	2 eggs

1 Cut the bread into neat dice and put into a basin.

2 If preferred make the bread into crumbs.

3 Heat the butter with the milk, pour over the bread.

4 Allow to cool slightly, then add the beaten eggs and most of the grated cheese.

5 Season well.

6 Pour into a pie or entrée dish and cover the top with the remainder of the cheese.

7 Bake for approximately 30–40 minutes in the centre of moderate oven (375°F.—Gas Mark 4) until firm.

Cheese tarts

cooking time   20 minutes

you will need:

cheese pastry (see page   seasoning
  83)   2 eggs
4 oz. grated cheese   1 gill milk

1 Line shallow patty tins with the pastry.
2 Beat the eggs and milk well together, add cheese and seasoning.
3 Spoon mixture into the pastry cases and bake for approximately 20 minutes in the centre of a moderately hot oven (400°F.—Gas Mark 5). Serve very hot.

Cheese and vegetable pie

cooking time   25 minutes

you will need:

8 oz. cheese   about 8 oz. runner beans
few carrots, peas, etc.   1½ oz. butter or
½ pint milk   margarine
few breadcrumbs   1½ oz. flour
small cauliflower   little extra butter

1 Prepare the vegetables.
2 Cook for about 15 minutes in boiling salted water until just tender.
3 Meanwhile grate the cheese.
4 Prepare the sauce. Melt butter in saucepan, combine with flour to make a smooth mixture.
5 Add milk slowly, stirring constantly, until thick and smooth.
6 Add 1 gill stock from the vegetables and cook together until well blended.
7 Season well.
8 Stir in 6 oz. cheese and all the vegetables.
9 Put into a hot pie dish and cover with the rest of the cheese, breadcrumbs and knobs of butter.
10 Brown under the grill.

Cheese soufflé

cooking time   approximately 30 minutes

you will need:

3 eggs   ¼ pint milk
1 oz. butter   3 oz. grated cheese*
½ oz. flour   salt and pepper
* Cheddar or mixture of Cheddar and Parmesan.

1 Separate the eggs.
2 Melt the butter and stir in the flour (for a firmer mixture use 1 oz. flour).
3 Gradually add the milk and bring to the boil, stirring until a smooth sauce.
4 Cool slightly.
5 Add cheese, seasoning and egg yolks one by one, beating well.
6 Fold in the very stiffly beaten egg whites.
7 Put into a prepared soufflé dish.
8 Bake in centre of a moderate oven (400°F.—

Gas Mark 5) for about 30 minutes, till well risen and brown.
9 Serve at once.

Cheese and potato pie

cooking time   10–20 minutes

1 Fill a casserole with slices of canned or cooked potatoes and canned sliced carrots.
2 Cover each layer with grated cheese.
3 Top with grated cheese or cheese sauce (see page 90).
4 Brown in the oven or under the grill.

Corn rarebit

cooking time   10 minutes

you will need:

1 gill, cooked canned or   seasoning—including 1
  frozen corn off the cob   teaspoon made mustard
1 teaspoon Worcester-   1 gill cooked but still firm
  shire sauce   cauliflower flowerets
¾ pint milk   8 oz. grated cheese
2 oz. flour   2 oz. butter
to garnish
grilled tomatoes   mushroom
toast

1 Heat the butter.
2 Stir in the flour.
3 Add the milk, and bring to the boil, stirring until a smooth thick sauce.
4 Add the cheese, allow to melt and season well.
5 Add the Worcestershire sauce.
6 Stir in the corn and cauliflower.
7 Serve with grilled tomatoes, mushrooms and crisp toast.

Frankfurter surprises

you will need:

8 slices fresh bread   2–3 oz. cream cheese
8 Frankfurter sausages   little pickle
watercress   butter

1 Spread the bread with little butter, cream cheese and chopped watercress.
2 Split each Frankfurter and spread with the pickle, then press halves together again.
3 Put at one end of the slices of bread and roll firmly.

Ham butterflies

cooking time   7–10 minutes

you will need:

cheese pastry (see   2 oz. ham
  page 83)   2 oz. butter

1 Cut the cheese pastry into small rounds and bake in a hot oven (425°F.—Gas Mark 6) for 7–10 minutes.
2 Cut up half of the rounds into semi-circles for 'wings'.
3 Make a spiced butter cream by creaming 2 oz.

butter with 2 oz. minced ham and spread over the rounds of cheese pastry.

4 Arrange the 2 semi-circles on top in the shape of wings and decorate with tiny rounds of olive or sprinkle lightly with paprika pepper.

Ham and apple turnovers

cooking time   40 minutes

you will need:

10 oz. short crust pastry	6 oz. cooked ham—cut in
(see page 63)	1 piece
little sugar	2 dessert apples

1 Cut out the pastry and cut into 4 large rounds.
2 Dice the ham and the apples and sprinkle with a little sugar.
3 Put on one half of the pastry, bring down the other half and seal the edges.
4 Flute together and bake for about 25 minutes on baking trays in the centre of a hot oven (450°F.—Gas Mark 7), reducing the heat after 15 minutes if the pastry is browning too much.

Macaroni cheese

cooking time   approximately 40 minutes for cooking macaroni and browning in oven

you will need:

3 oz. macaroni	1 tablespoon crisp
$\frac{1}{2}$ pint cheese sauce	breadcrumbs
(see page 90)	1 oz. margarine or butter
2 oz. grated cheese	

* If you like a more moist macaroni cheese, then use $\frac{3}{4}$ pint cheese sauce to the same quantity of cooked macaroni.

1 Put the macaroni into about $1\frac{1}{2}$ pints boiling water, to which you have added 1 level teaspoon salt.
2 Cook steadily until the macaroni is just tender.
3 Do not overcook, elbow-length quick-cooking macaroni takes only 7 minutes.
4 Drain in a colander, arrange it in a hot dish and pour the cheese sauce over it.
5 Sprinkle cheese and breadcrumbs on top and put the margarine or butter on in several small pieces.
6 Either bake for about 25 minutes near the top of a moderately hot oven (400°F.—Gas Mark 5) until crisp and brown, or put under a hot grill.
7 To get rid of starchiness of macaroni it can be rinsed under hot tap before using.

Picnic patties

cooking time   30 minutes

you will need:

8 oz. short crust pastry (see page 63)
filling

egg	1 gill milk
8 oz. prepared shrimps	2 oz. grated cheese
(or chopped ham)	salt and pepper

1 Divide the pastry into 4 and roll out each piece on a lightly floured board to a round large enough to line 4 foil baking cases or deep patty tins $3\frac{1}{2}$–4 inches in diameter.
2 Press well down into the cases.
3 Trim, flake and flute the pastry cases.
4 Prick the bottoms.

To make the filling

1 Place the egg and milk in a basin and whisk together.
2 Add the shrimps or ham, cheese, salt and pepper and mix together.
3 Place the lined foil cases on a baking sheet, fill with the mixture.
4 Bake on the second shelf from the top of a moderately hot oven (400°F.—Gas Mark 5) 25–30 minutes.
5 Cool on a wire tray.

Poached egg and spinach

1 Poached eggs and spinach are a perfect partnership.
2 Cook spinach, drain well and top with poached egg.
3 To make a more substantial meal coat with cheese sauce (see page 90).

Potato loaf·

cooking time   45 minutes

you will need:

crisp breadcrumbs	butter or margarine
1 lb. cooked new	8 oz. tomatoes—skinned
potatoes—cut into	and sliced
thick slices	
cheese sauce	
1 oz. margarine or	1 oz. flour
butter	$\frac{1}{3}$ pint milk
seasoning	parsley for garnishing
4 oz. grated cheese	

1 Coat the tin liberally with margarine or butter.
2 Shake over the crumbs.
3 Arrange layers of the sliced potatoes and tomatoes.
4 Cover each layer with some of the thick well-flavoured cheese sauce.
5 Cover the dish well with greased paper and bake for about 45 minutes in the centre of a moderate oven (375°F.—Gas Mark 4).
6 Turn out and serve with crisp watercress and cauliflower.

Puffy cottage cheese omelette with quick mushroom sauce

cooking time   approximately 10 minutes

you will need:

4 eggs, separated	sprinkle of pepper
8 oz. cottage cheese	¼ teaspoon salt
1 oz. butter	

1 Beat egg yolks, pepper and salt until creamy.
2 Beat in cottage cheese.
3 Whisk egg whites until stiff but not dry.
4 Fold into egg mixture.
5 Melt butter in pan (about 10-inch is best).
6 Pour in omelette mixture, spreading evenly.
7 Cook slowly for about 10 minutes, loosening sides with round-topped knife and shaking very gently to loosen bottom.
8 Serve at once with quick mushroom sauce.
9 Delicious with hot asparagus for special occasions.

Quick mushroom sauce

Heat condensed mushroom soup from a small can and stir in gill cultured cream (commercially soured cream or use cream and 1 dessertspoon lemon juice).

Salmon loaf

you will need:

medium-sized can salmon	3 oz. finely diced cucumber
2 hard-boiled eggs	
8 oz. diced cooked new potatoes	seasoning
	little chopped parsley
crisp lettuce	mayonnaise
sliced cucumber	tomatoes

1 Put the salmon, chopped eggs, diced cucumber, potatoes and parsley into a basin.
2 Mix with seasoning and a little mayonnaise.
3 Press into greased loaf tin and leave in the refrigerator or cool place for several hours.
4 Turn out carefully on to a bed of crisp lettuce.
5 Garnish with cucumber and tomatoes.

Scotch eggs

cooking time   15 minutes plus time for boiling eggs

you will need:

4 eggs	1 egg for coating
2 tablespoons flour	½ gill milk for coating
12 oz. sausage meat	deep fat for frying
breadcrumbs	

1 Hard-boil the eggs and cool them. Shell them.
2 Roll them lightly in flour.
3 Divide the sausage meat into 4, fold evenly and smooth round the lightly floured eggs.
4 Coat these with the beaten egg and milk blended together, roll each firmly in breadcrumbs.

5 Fry steadily in fat and drain.
6 Remember that the sausage meat has to cook so do not hurry the frying process.
7 Cut each Scotch egg in half with a sharp knife dipped in hot water.
8 Serve hot with tomato sauce (see page 89) or cold with salad.

Spring casserole

cooking time   20 minutes

you will need:

1 can condensed chicken soup or creamy white sauce (see page 90)	4 hard-boiled eggs
	2 6½ oz. cans asparagus
	½ teaspoon made mustard

1 Slice the hard-boiled eggs.
2 Arrange the slices with the asparagus in a greased fireproof dish.
3 Combine the soup or sauce with the mustard.
4 Pour over the contents of the dish.
5 Bake for 20 minutes in a hot oven or until the asparagus is tender.

Tomato fish cakes

cooking time   5–8 minutes

you will need:

2 large fresh or well-drained canned tomatoes	8–10 oz. cooked cod or fresh haddock
	1 small egg
8 oz. cooked mashed potatoes	crisp breadcrumbs
	seasoning
fat for frying	

1 Skin and chop the tomatoes very finely, mix with the potatoes and fish, season well.
2 Form into 8 small cakes, coat with the egg and crumbs and fry in shallow fat.
3 For extra economy use the egg yolk only with a small amount of water or milk for coating the fish cakes and save the whites for macaroons or meringues.

Welsh rarebit

cooking time   approximately 10 minutes

you will need:

4–6 large slices of toast	butter for toast
8 oz. cheese	salt
1 teaspoon made mustard	pepper
	1 oz. butter
1 tablespoon beer or ale or Worcestershire sauce	1 oz. flour
	1 gill milk

1 Heat the butter in a saucepan, stir in the flour and cook steadily for several minutes, then gradually add the cold milk.
2 Bring to the boil and cook until smooth and thick.

3 Add the mustard, salt, pepper, most of the cheese and beer.
4 Heat steadily, without boiling too quickly, until the cheese has melted.
5 Spread over the hot buttered toast, sprinkle with the remainder of the cheese and brown under a hot grill. Serve at once. This Welsh rarebit mixture can be stored in covered jars for some days in a refrigerator.

Tomato Rarebit
Blend the mixture with tomato juice or soup instead of milk. If using soup use a little less flour.

Celery Rarebit
Arrange neat pieces of well drained cooked celery on the toast and coat with the Welsh rarebit mixture. The celery stock can be used instead of milk.

Buck Rarebit
Top the mixture with a poached egg.

Creole Rarebit
Mix the rarebit mixture with fried onion and tomatoes and little corn on the cob.

Vegetable Rarebit
Mix the rarebit mixture with few cooked well drained vegetables.

York Rarebit
Ingredients and method as Welsh rarebit, but put a thick slice of cooked ham on each piece of toast, cover with the cheese mixture.

To make good salads
All the ingredients should be as fresh as possible for a salad since you lose both vitamin value and a good appearance if they are limp. Salads vary a great deal in the ingredients that are put into them. Today it is accepted that one can mix fruit, nuts, etc. in with green lettuce, etc. for a salad. In the same way it is perfectly correct, and very popular, to serve a cold salad with hot, grilled or roasted dishes.

To prepare ingredients for salads
1 Lettuce—endive, cabbage and all other green vegetables, should be well washed and dried.
2 If shredding make sure you have a stainless silver knife so they are not discoloured.
3 Do not shred too soon before serving the salad.

1 Cucumber—can be peeled or not according to personal taste.
2 To give an attractive effect to the peel, score the skin by dragging the point of the fork down very firmly.

1 Tomatoes—can be skinned by lowering carefully into hot water for a minute and then into cold water.
2 They can then be sliced.
3 If the skin is left on, cut into water lily shapes. To do this use a sharp knife.

Insert the point of the knife into the tomato and cut into a Vandyke pattern through the tomato, each time feeling the knife going through to the centre.
When you have completed doing this pull the tomato gently apart and you have 2 halves of a water lily.

1 Radishes—Wash, dry and slice.
2 Or cut into water lilies as for tomatoes.
3 Or with practice you can make more elaborate shapes by cutting the actual skin away from the centre of the radish in petal shapes.
4 If time permits though; the easiest way to make a flower is to cut the radish from the top into about 8 sections.
5 Don't cut right down to the bottom.
6 Put into very cold water for an hour or so and these will open up.

1 Celery—should either be diced or cut into thin strips.
2 Then put into iced or cold water when the strips will form celery curls.

Cheese salads
Many types of cheese are ideal for salads.
1 Try grating *Cheddar,* or *Cheshire* or *Lancashire.*
2 Or have a soft *cream cheese,* or if slimming try *cottage cheese.*
3 *Blue* or *Stilton cheese* can be served in salads—dice or crumble these.
4 Arrange the salad on a bed of lettuce, top with mayonnaise if wished and garnish with sliced cucumber, tomatoes, etc.
5 Remember though that fruit combines well with cheese in a salad. Rings of pineapples, apple or orange are delicious, and so are dates or walnuts.

Egg salads

Hard-boiled eggs can be served in salads whole or in halves.

1 To give a more unusual salad halve the eggs carefully.
2 Remove the yolks and mash with butter or mayonnaise and seasoning.
3 These can then be blended with chutney or curry powder, chopped shrimps or prawns, diced ham, or with grated cheese.
4 The yolk is then piled back into the white case.
5 Serve on a bed of lettuce, or cress garnished with radishes, cucumber, tomato, etc.
6 Although *hard-boiled* eggs are generally used as a basis for salads, well-flavoured *scrambled egg* could be used instead. Garnish with chopped chives and/or parsley.

Fish salads

Most fish is excellent in salads.
If using shell fish—lobster, prawns, crab, etc.

1 They are prepared either by shelling, or removing the meat from the shells.
2 Mixing with mayonnaise.
3 Serve on a bed of lettuce, etc.
4 CRAB and LOBSTER can be served in the shells.
5 Be careful to remove the stomach from crab and the grey fingers—and the intestinal vein and stomach from lobster.
6 The claws are cracked, and the meat removed from these and arranged either beside the shell or mixed with the meat in the shells.

If using white fish
1 Cook carefully, taking care not to over-cook.
2 Make into rather large flakes.
3 Blend with mayonnaise and pile into pyramid shapes on the green salad.
4 It can be mixed with a little shell fish.

If using oily fish
Herrings and mackerel are excellent in salads.
1 They can be grilled or fried.
2 Then blend the flesh flakes with a little oil and vinegar and seasoning in a salad.
3 An even better way though is to SOUSE the fish.
4 Cook in equal quantities of vinegar and water.
5 Add seasonings, spices to taste and cook slowly until the fish is tender.
6 Allow to cool in the liquid.

Meat salads

1 Any cooked meat—ham, tongue, salami, joints of beef, etc., are delicious with salads.
2 Remember not to leave the sliced meat exposed to the air too long, for it dries easily, and loses both taste and attractive appearance.
3 For special occasions have large dishes with a selection of many different kinds of cold meat arranged on a bed of mixed salad.

Orange salad

you will need:

2 large oranges	good pinch salt
lettuce	pepper, sugar
1½ tablespoons oil	1 small teaspoon
1½ tablespoons vinegar	mustard

1 Wash and dry lettuce and arrange on small plates.
2 Peel oranges and remove outside pith then, using a very sharp knife, cut sections from the orange.
3 Arrange on the lettuce.
4 Put the mustard on to a flat plate, add the seasonings, and gradually blend in the oil and vinegar.
5 Pour over the salad.

Cheese shortbreads

cooking time   15 minutes

you will need:

4 oz. flour (with plain flour use approximately ½ teaspoon baking powder)	few halved almonds good pinch salt celery salt mustard
2 oz. grated cheese	2½ oz. margarine

1 Cream margarine and cheese.
2 Sieve flour and seasonings, add to the margarine.
3 Form into small balls. If rather sticky roll with DAMP (not too wet) hands.
4 Put on to greased trays.
5 Decorate with halved almonds.
6 Allow space to spread out.
7 Bake for 15 minutes in centre of moderate oven (375°F.—Gas Mark 4).

Water biscuits

cooking time   8 minutes

you will need:

8 oz. flour	½ teaspoon salt
1 oz. butter	water

1 Sieve flour and salt together.
2 Rub in butter.
3 Add enough water to bind.
4 Roll out until very thin, i.e. like ice cream wafers.
5 Cut into rounds.
6 Put on to an ungreased baking tin and bake near top of moderately hot oven (425°F.—Gas Mark 6) for about 8 minutes.

Chapter 14
Sauces and Stuffings

In this chapter you will find recipes for simple sauces and stuffings. These make all the difference to the appeal of many dishes, and are an economy measure as well. A stuffed piece of meat goes quite a bit further than one without stuffing.

Apple sauce

you will need:

1 lb. apples	2 tablespoons sugar
1 oz. margarine or butter	water

1 Peel and core apples and slice thinly.
2 Put into small saucepan adding about 1 gill of water, the margarine and the sugar.
3 Beat well with wooden spoon when apples are cooked to give a good appearance.

Bread sauce

you will need:

3 oz. breadcrumbs	1–2 oz. margarine or butter
1 small onion	
½ pint milk	2 or 3 cloves, if liked
salt	pepper

1 Peel the onion and if using cloves stick these firmly into the onion.
2 Put this into the milk together with the other ingredients and slowly bring milk to the boil.
3 Remove from the heat and stand in a warm place for as long as possible, for if the mixture is not allowed to stand and infuse, the bread sauce is sadly lacking in flavour.
4 Heat sauce again gently, beating well with wooden spoon, just before meal is ready.
5 Remove onion before putting into sauce boat.

Caper sauce

cooking time   7–10 minutes

you will need:

1 oz. butter or margarine	1 oz. flour
½ pint milk*	seasoning
½–1 tablespoon capers	few drops vinegar from the capers

* Since caper sauce is often served with boiled mutton or lamb a better flavour results if half milk is used and half meat stock.

Proceed as white sauce (see page 90), adding the capers and vinegar when the sauce is cooked.

Condensed milk mayonnaise

you will need:

1 gill sweetened condensed milk	2 tablespoons oil
	½ teaspoon salt
2 tablespoons vinegar or lemon juice	¼ teaspoon cayenne pepper
	½ teaspoon dry mustard

1 Gradually mix all the ingredients together.
2 You may like to increase the amount of vinegar to give a more tart flavour.

Cranberry sauce

you will need:

12 oz. cranberries	1 tablespoon port wine (not essential)
3 oz. sugar	
¾ gill water	

Heat water and sugar together, add the fruit and cook until tender. Add port (or sherry) if wished.

Orange and port wine sauce

1 Peel 2 oranges and remove white pith from the skin. Cut this into very narrow ribbons.
2 Simmer in a little water until tender.
3 Make brown sauce with stock from giblets.
4 Add a little port wine and the orange strips.
5 To serve with duck or goose.

Tomato sauce

cooking time   approximately 30 minutes

you will need:

5 large fresh or canned tomatoes	1 small onion
	bay leaf
½ pint stock or liquid from can	1 oz. butter
	½ oz. flour
1 rasher bacon	salt and pepper
good pinch sugar	1 carrot

1 Dice the onion, carrot and bacon.
2 Heat the butter and toss them in this—do not brown.
3 Add tomatoes and simmer for a few minutes with canned tomatoes and rather longer with fresh tomatoes.
4 Take time doing this, since it improves the flavour of the sauce.
5 Blend the flour with the stock, add to the ingredients and simmer gently for about 30 minutes.
6 Stir from time to time.
7 Rub through a sieve or beat with a wooden spoon, add seasoning and sugar.
8 The bay leaf can be put in at the same time as the tomatoes, but for a milder flavour add with the stock.

9 For a vegetarian sauce omit the bacon. Garlic or garlic salt can be added.

Quick tomato sauce

cooking time   approximately 10 minutes

you will need:

1 small tube or can tomato purée	salt and pepper
1 oz. butter or margarine	1 small apple
2 level teaspoons cornflour	1 small onion
	$\frac{1}{2}$ pint water
	good pinch sugar

1 Peel and grate both the onion and the apple.
2 Heat the butter and fry the onion for a few minutes, then the apple.
3 Add the purée, the cornflour blended with the water and seasoning.
4 Bring to the boil and stir until smooth.
5 Simmer gently for about 10 minutes, taste and re-season and add sugar if wished.

Tartare sauce (cold)

(To serve with fish salads, particularly fresh salmon)

you will need:

$\frac{1}{2}$ gill mayonnaise or salad dressing	$\frac{1}{2}$ teaspoon capers
$\frac{1}{2}$ tablespoon finely chopped gherkin or cucumber	few drops vinegar or lemon juice
	1 teaspoon finely chopped parsley

Mix all ingredients together, stirring briskly.

Economical tartare sauce (hot)

cooking time   12 minutes

you will need:

$\frac{1}{2}$ pint white sauce (see below)	seasoning
1 tablespoon vinegar or lemon juice	1 egg
2 teaspoons chopped parsley	2 teaspoons chopped gherkins
	1–2 teaspoons chopped capers

1 Make the white sauce in the usual way, making certain it is well cooked and thickened.
2 Remove the sauce from the heat, and whisk in the beaten egg and lemon juice.
3 Return to a *very low heat,* and cook gently for approximately 3–4 minutes, taking care the mixture does not boil and curdle.
4 Stir in the parsley, capers and gherkins and extra seasoning, if required.

White sauce

cooking time   7–10 minutes

you will need:

1 oz. butter or margarine	1 oz. flour
	pepper

$\frac{1}{2}$ pint milk for coating consistency i.e. sauce	1 gill milk for panada or binding consistency
1 pint milk for thin white sauce for soups	salt

1 Heat the butter gently, remove from the heat and stir in flour.
2 Return to the heat and cook gently for a few minutes so the 'roux' as the butter and flour mixture is called, does not brown.
3 Again remove the pan from the heat and gradually blend in the cold milk.
4 Bring to the boil and cook, stirring with a wooden spoon, until smooth.
5 Season well. If any small lumps have formed whisk sharply.

Variations on white sauce

Cheese sauce
1 Stir in 3–6 oz. grated cheese.
2 When sauce has thickened, add mustard.
3 Serve with vegetable, meat, fish and savoury dishes.

Parsley sauce
1 Add 1–2 teaspoons chopped parsley.
2 Serve with fish, etc.

Prawn or shrimp sauce
1 Make white sauce.
2 Add about $\frac{1}{2}$–1 gill chopped prawns and a little anchovy essence just before serving.
3 If using fresh prawns, simmer shells and use stock instead of the same amount of milk.
4 Serve with fish.

Apple and onion stuffing

you will need:

3 good-sized cooking apples	$\frac{1}{2}$ teaspoon grated lemon rind
4 good-sized onions	pinch thyme
8 oz. cooked potatoes	salt
$\frac{1}{2}$ teaspoon dried sage	pepper

1 Peel the apples and chop very finely.
2 Chop the onion and cook for a short time.
3 Mix all ingredients together and season well.
4 Serve with goose, duck or pork.

Chestnut stuffing

you will need:

1 lb. chestnuts	seasoning
3 oz. breadcrumbs	$\frac{1}{2}$ gill milk
1 or 2 oz. margarine	

1 Boil the chestnuts until soft.
2 Remove shells and rub nuts through a sieve.
3 Add to the breadcrumbs, together with seasoning, margarine and milk.
4 Serve with turkey or chicken.

Forcemeat stuffing

you will need:

8 oz. sausage meat	1 egg
chopped parsley	mixed herbs

1 Mix all ingredients thoroughly.
2 If desired, the finely chopped cooked giblets of the poultry can be added.
3 This quantity is enough for a chicken.
4 For a turkey use twice as much, use it for one end and put chestnut stuffing (see preceding recipe) at the other.

Fried crumbs

1 Make large crumbs from bread.
2 Fry in butter until crisp and golden brown.
3 This can be done the day before and the crumbs reheated gently in the oven.

Ham and rice stuffing

you will need:

8 oz. rice	2 teaspoons chopped
4–6 oz. chopped ham	parsley
or bacon	1 teaspoon mixed herbs
2 oz. butter	1 egg
seasoning	chopped cooked liver of
5 oz. celery or large	the bird
onion	

1 Boil the rice in salted water until just tender.
2 Chop celery or onion finely and fry in the hot butter.
3 Add to the rice (which should be well drained) together with the other ingredients.

Sage and onion stuffing

you will need:

2 large onions (peeled)	3 oz. breadcrumbs
1 teaspoon dried sage	1 oz. suet or butter
1 egg	good pinch salt and
about $\frac{1}{2}$ pint water	pepper

1 Put the onions into a saucepan, adding water.
2 Simmer steadily for about 20 minutes, when the onions will be partly cooked.
3 Remove from water on to chopping board and chop into small pieces.
4 Transfer to a basin and then add all other ingredients.
5 Add a little onion stock if wished.
6 This is sufficient for a duck—for a large goose use about 3 times the quantity.

Veal stuffing

you will need:

4 oz. breadcrumbs	1 egg
2–3 teaspoons chopped	2 oz. shredded suet or
parsley	melted margarine
grated rind and juice	$\frac{1}{2}$ teaspoon mixed herbs
of $\frac{1}{2}$ lemon	

1 Mix all the ingredients together thoroughly.
2 The cooked meat from the giblets can be added to make a rich stuffing, if wished.
3 Make 2 or 3 times this quantity for a large turkey.

Giblet stuffing

As for veal stuffing but instead of parsley use the finely chopped cooked giblets of the bird.

Index